A
HISTORY OF
EVERYDAY THINGS
IN ENGLAND

EVERYDAY THINGS IN ENGLAND
Vol.   I.   1066-1499.
Vol. II.   1500-1799.
Vol. III.   1733-1851.
Vol. IV.   1852-1914.
   Demy 8vo.

" EVERYDAY LIFE " SERIES
Vol.   I.   Everyday Life in the Old Stone Age.
Vol. II.   Everyday Life in the New Stone Age, Bronze and Early Iron Age.
Vols. I and II together : Everyday Life in Prehistoric Times.
Vol. III.   Everyday Life in Roman Britain.
Vol. IV.   Life in Saxon, Viking and Norman Times.
   Crown 8vo.

EVERYDAY THINGS IN ANCIENT GREECE
   Revised by Kathleen Freeman.
   Demy 8vo.

EVERYDAY LIFE IN NEW TESTAMENT TIMES
   By A. C. Bouquet.
   With illustrations by Marjorie Quennell.
   Demy 8vo.

FIG. 1.—A Banquet at the Royal Pavilion, Brighton.

(From the coloured lithograph by Joseph Nash.)

A
HISTORY OF
EVERYDAY THINGS
IN ENGLAND

Volume III
1733 to 1851

By

MARJORIE & C. H. B. QUENNELL

LONDON
B. T. BATSFORD LTD

TO THE MEMORY OF
THE REV. JAMES WOODFORDE
WHO KEPT A DIARY FROM
1758 TO 1803

TO JOHN BERESFORD
WHO DISCOVERED IT

TO THE OXFORD UNIVERSITY PRESS
WHO PUBLISHED IT

FIRST PUBLISHED, 1933
SIXTH IMPRESSION, 1954

MADE AND PRINTED IN GREAT BRITAIN BY
TONBRIDGE PRINTERS LTD., SHIPBOURNE ROAD, TONBRIDGE
FOR THE PUBLISHERS
B. T. BATSFORD LTD.
4 FITZHARDINGE STREET, PORTMAN SQUARE
LONDON, W.I

PREFACE

THE boys and girls for whom we write will know that we are mainly concerned with showing people at work, and that it does not matter what the work is so long as it is interesting—and we might add if work is natural and proper then it cannot be uninteresting. For example, take cleaning out a cattle-yard deep in manure. If you are a farmer or gardener you will be looking ahead to the crops which you will grow with the aid of the manure, and the smelly job becomes interesting.

It will be found that work divides itself quite naturally into three great trades. Men must eat, so the farmer's trade is the most important one. It does not matter whether the breakfast bacon comes from Denmark, or the dinner's mutton from New Zealand, the cheese from Canada, and the eggs from China, it is the farmer who feeds you ; and though the food may be packed in a tin, this was not its natal couch. The farmer grows the raw materials also for the second great trade of Clothing. The fleeces of his sheep are woven into cloth ; the hides of his cattle make shoes, and the flax he grows, the linen. The third great trade is the Builder's—he provides the houses. All the other trades are subsidiary and relatively unimportant, as can be seen in the chart on the opposite page.

Until the end of the eighteenth century we carried on these three great trades by ourselves for ourselves, and with the surplus over and beyond our needs paid for luxuries, like wine, which we imported. In the nineteenth century, from a variety of causes, all of which seemed very reasonable, this natural balance began to be disturbed. The emigrants who went to America and Australia sent home for the goods which they could not manufacture themselves, and paid us for them with foodstuffs grown on virgin soils. More and more it began to pay us to manufacture these goods, and so this Industrial Revolution altered our mode of living—it was rooted in money instead of in the land.

The idea of this book is to contrast these two modes of living—the simple natural methods of the eighteenth century, which first began in England when Neolithic man planted his crops on the lynchets and tended his flocks on the Downs, and the modern Industrialism, which is so recent, and difficult, and complicated. We cannot of course do more than touch on the many problems with which Man has been confronted, but we shall pay especial attention to the difficulties which he has had to overcome. Man is a cantankerous animal, very frequently wrong-headed and perverse ; he will run a heel-line with the greatest joy and cause his friends despair, but he is ingenious and skilful—so much must be admitted. We will show him exhibiting his ingenuity and skill.

MARJORIE and C. H. B. QUENNELL.

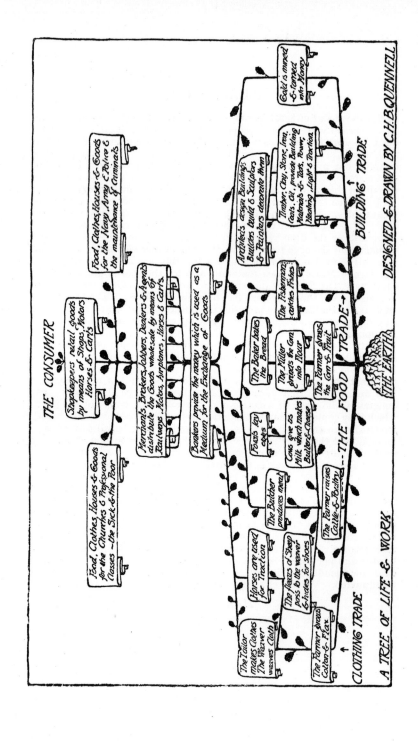

THE CONSUMER

Food, Clothes, Houses & Goods for the Navy, Army & Police & the maintenance of Criminals

Shopkeepers retail goods by means of Shops, Motors, Horses & Carts

Food, Clothes, Houses & Goods for the Churches & Professional Classes —the Sick & the Poor

Merchants, Brokers, Jobbers, Dealers & Agents distribute the Goods wholesale by means of Railways, Motors, Airplanes, Horses & Carts

Bankers provide the money which is used as a Medium for the Exchange of Goods

Architects design Buildings Builders build & Sculptors & Painters decorate them

Timber, Clay, Stone, Iron, Coals, Air, private Building Materials & Tar, Power, Heating, Light & Traction

Gold is mined & stamped into Money

The Fisherman catches Fishes

The Baker bakes the Bread

The Miller grinds the Corn into Flour

The Farmer grows the Corn & Fruit

Fowls lay eggs

Cows give us Milk which makes Butter & Cheese

The Butcher produces meat

The Farmer raises Cattle & Poultry

Horses are used for Traction

The Fleeces of Sheep pass to the weaver & hides for shoes

The Tailor makes Clothes The Weaver weaves Cloth

The Farmer grows Cotton & Flax

CLOTHING TRADE

...THE FOOD TRADE—

BUILDING TRADE

THE EARTH

A TREE OF LIFE & WORK

DESIGNED & DRAWN BY C.H.B.QUENNELL

CONTENTS

LIST OF ILLUSTRATIONS

LIST OF ILLUSTRATIONS

ix

LIST OF ILLUSTRATIONS

LIST OF ILLUSTRATIONS

SHORT LIST OF AUTHORITIES

Rural Rides. WILLIAM COBBETT.
Agricultural Implements and Machinery. SPENCER and PASSMORE.
Under Eight Reigns. BERTRAM HELLYER.
The Works of Sir John Soane. A. T. BOLTON.
Ancient Egyptian and Greek Looms. H. LING ROTH.
Primitive Looms. H. LING ROTH.
The Wheelwright's Shop. GEORGE STURT.
Country Life.
" Travel " and " Clothing." By Col. F. S. BRERETON.
Road Transport. E. A. FORWARD.
Railway Locomotives. E. A. FORWARD.
Merchant Steamers. G. S. LAIRD CLOWES.
Sailing Ships. G. S. LAIRD CLOWES.
Stationary Engines. H. W. DICKINSON.
The Log of the *Cutty Sark.* BASIL LUBBOCK.
The Diary of a Country Parson. JAMES WOODFORDE. Ed. by JOHN
    BERESFORD.
History of American Government and Culture. H. RUGG.
History of American Invention. Ed. by W. KAEMPFFERT.
The Horse-Hoing Husbandry. JETHRO TULL.
The Farington Diary. Ed. by J. GREIG.
The Smaller English House, 1660–1830. RICHARDSON and EBERLEIN.
English Interiors, 1660–1830. M. JOURDAIN.
Smaller Houses of Late Georgian Period. S. C. RAMSEY.
British History in the Nineteenth Century, and After, 1782–1919. G. M.
    TREVELYAN.
English Social History : A Survey of Six Centuries, Chaucer to Queen
    Victoria. G. M. TREVEYLAN.
The Age of Adam. J. LEES-MILNE.
The Regency Style. DONALD PILCHER.
Early Victorian England, 1830–1865, 2 vols. G. M. YOUNG (editor).
Regency and Early Victorian Times. E. BERESFORD CHANCELLOR.
English Women's Clothing in the 19th Century. C. WILLETT CUNNINGTON.
British Architects & Craftsmen, 1600–1830. SACHEVERELL SITWELL.
Stuart and Georgian Churches, 1603–1837. MARCUS WHIFFEN.
Change in the Farm. T. HENNELL.
The Railways of Britain. O. S. NOCK.
The Smaller English House. REGINALD TURNOR.
Travel in England. THOMAS BURKE.
The English Interior. RALPH DUTTON.
Nineteenth Century Architecture in Britain. REGINALD TURNOR.
The Bridges of Britain. ERIC DE MARÉ.
English Sports and Pastimes. CHRISTINA HOLE.
English Home Life. CHRISTINA HOLE.
British Trains : Past and Present. O. S. NOCK.
English Town Crafts. NORMAN WYMER.
Outline of English Architecture. A. H. GARDNER.
A History of Flying. C. H. GIBBS-SMITH.

CHART I.

Kings, Political, and Social	Science and Industry	Art
1727 GEORGE II.	1724 Turnips first used for cattle	
		1726 " Gulliver's Travels " (Swift)
		1727 Kent's book on Architecture
		Chiswick Villa
		1728 Gibbs' boon on Architecture
1732 Birth of George Washing-ton	1730 Townshend turns to agriculture	
	1732 Birth of Richard Arkwright	
	1733 Tull's horse-hoing husbandry	
	Kay's flying shuttle	
	introduce Industrialism	
		1734 Holkham started and foundation of Dilettanti Society
1737 Death of Queen Caroline	1740 Foundation of London Hospital	1740 " Pamela " published
	1741 Death of Tull	
	Birth of Arthur Young	
		1742 Batty Langley's " Gothic Architecture Restored and Improved"
1743 Dettingen	1745 Bakewell begins	1745 Lord Dacre gothicizes Belhus
1746 Culloden		
1747		1747 Woburn Abbey
1748 Henry Fielding at Bow Street		1748 " Roderick Random " published
	1750-7 Hargreaves designs his jenny	1750 Prior Park, Bath
		Walpole builds Strawberry Hill
		1751 Prison series, Piranesi
		1753 Foundation Society of Arts
		Chinese buildings by Chambers
1755 Seven Years' War	1754 Railways (not loco.) at Bath	
1757		1755 Johnson's Dictionary
		1758 Robert Adam returns from Italy
1759 Wolfe's victory, Heights of Abraham	1759 Eddystone Lighthouse (Smeaton)	1759 Chambers' " Civil Architecture "
	Washington farming at Mt. Vernon	
1760 GEORGE III.		1760 " Tristram Shandy " published
	1761 Brindley's canals	1761 Kedlestone, Derbyshire
		1762 Stuart and Revett's " Antiquities of Athens "
1763 Peace with France	1763 Watt begins on steam engine and Wedgwood starts pottery	1763 Chinese work at Kew, Chambers
1765 Population of England and Wales 7,000,000		
		1766 " Vicar of Wakefield " published
		" Antiquites Etrusque Greques et Romaine "
1767		1768 Adelphi, London
	1769 Arkwright's spinning machine	1769 Foundation of Royal Academy
	Wedgwood opens Etruria	
1771	1770 Cugnot's experiments	1770 Newgate begun
1773 Johnson's journey to the Hebrides	Birth of Trevithick	
		1773 Works in Architecture (Adam)
1773 Boston Tea Riots		" She Stoops to Conquer " published
1775 Bunker's Hill	1774-9 Crompton's mule	
1776 Declaration of Independence, U.S.A.	1775 Cumming's closet	
	1776 Coke of Holkham begins farming and starts the Holkham Meetings, 1778	1776 Somerset House, London
	Adam Smith's " Wealth of Nations "	
1777	Jenner vaccinates	
1780 Gordon Riots	1780 Robinson's range	1779 Coalbrookdale Bridge
1781 Surrender of Cornwallis, Yorktown	1781 Trade very bad	1780 Finsbury Square, London
	Watt perfects steam engine	
1782 Rodney's victory	Birth of George Stephenson	
1783 Peace with America, France and Spain	1783 Montgolfier balloons	
		1784 Brighton Pavilion begun (Holland)
	1785 Cartwright's Power Loom	
		1786 First edition Burns' poems
		Carlton House, London (Holland)
1787		
	1788 Bramah's closet	1788 Ayot St. Lawrence Church
		Soane made architect Bank of England
	1791 Birth of Faraday	
		1792 Death of Robert Adam
1793 France declares war on England	1793 Young becomes Secretary of Board of Agriculture	
Execution of Louis XVI.		
1795		1795 Southill, Beds. (Holland)
1796 Powder Tax		
1797 Speenhamland decision	1797 Trevithick makes his model loco.	
1799	Soane uses steam heating	

Chart II.—George III to Victoria, 1799–1851, p. 108

PART I

CHAPTER I

THE EIGHTEENTH-CENTURY FARMER

W HEN we look back on life as lived on this island of ours, up till the end of the eighteenth century, it seems to us to have been very comfortable and easy. Doubtless our forbears had their troubles, but they did have time to grapple with them. The first known Englishman, was a hunter of strange animals in Sussex, and his followers in the New Stone Age guarded their flocks on the chalk Downs, and grew corn on the narrow lynchets. The Bronze Age Men and those of the Early Iron Age, if they came as invaders, stayed to be absorbed into the stock. The Romans tried to teach us Townplanning, and made roads before we understood their meaning ; we were part of a mighty empire that stretched from Babylon to Britain. Then the Dark Ages descended, and Angles, Saxons and Jutes wandered through the ruins of Silchester, but preferred to make clearings for their own houses in the woods. The Normans brought us the vigour of the North once more, and the culture they had absorbed in Normandy, and then, under the Angevins, we again became part of an empire that included all the Western parts of France. But gradually our outlook became more insular, and so we came to the Renaissance and the discovery of the New World. Adventurers went there, and we contested with the Spaniards on the West Indian seas, but the placid stream of life at home flowed on, and there was little alteration in the colour of our thoughts or the mode of our living ; and so things remained until the beginning of the eighteenth century. Then came a series of happenings which brought the Industrial

I

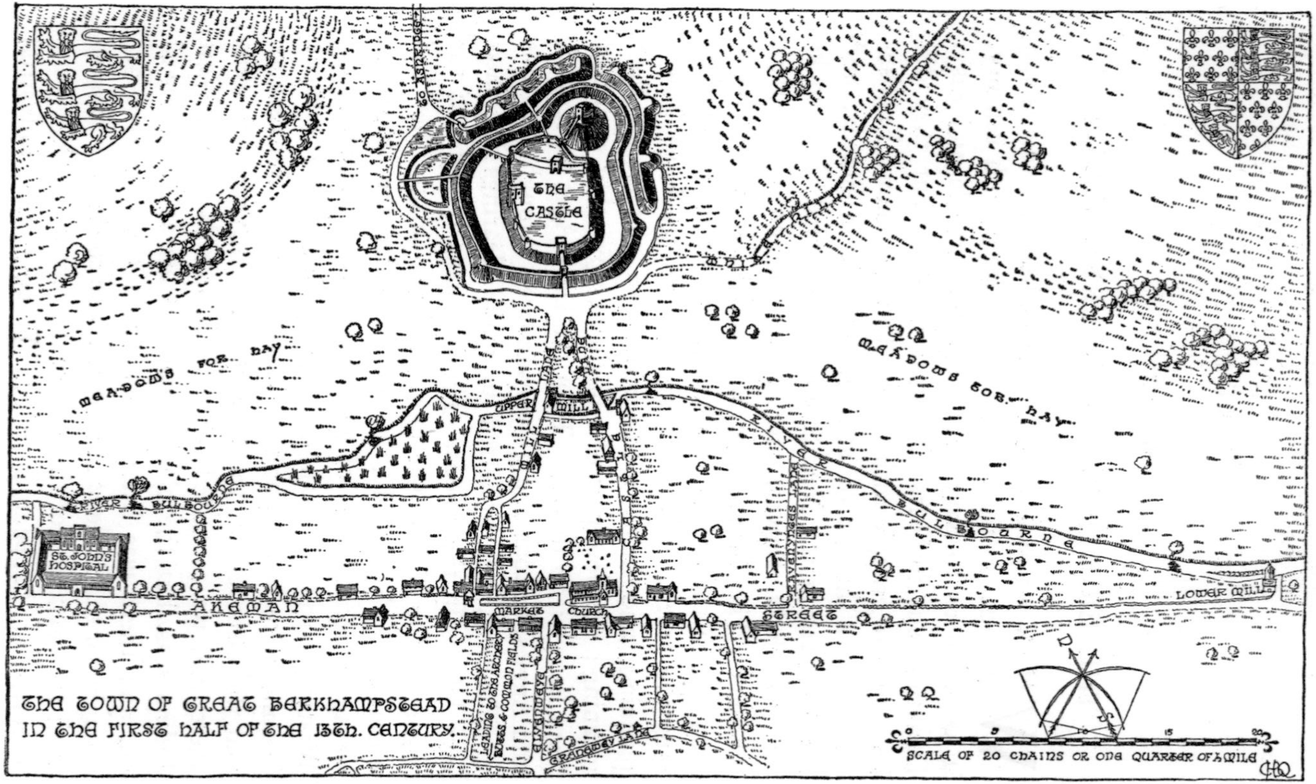
The Town of Great Berkhampstead
in the First Half of the 13th. Century.
The Castle
To Ashridge
Meadows for hay
Meadows for hay
Upper Mill
River Bulbourne
River Bulbourne
St. John's Hospital
Akeman
Street
Market
Church
Lower Mill
Leading to the Archery Butts & Common Fields
Granaway Lane
Scale of 20 chains or one quarter of a mile
0
5
15
20

FIG. 3.

Revolution in its train, and time became a kind of fourth dimension which could not be grappled with. Tull introduced new ideas which revolutionized agriculture, James Watt's monster was born. Bridgewater made canals, and Macadam, roads, and we were hardly used to these when Stephenson's iron horse ran on rails instead of roads. Industrial towns sprang up and introduced unheard-of complications of Town Planning and Sanitation. Problems to which a thousand years had gone to find a solution had to be settled in as many weeks. So we must be very charitable in dealing with the Industrial Revolution.

The first of the three great trades to be affected by the change was that of the farmer, but before we deal with the revolution in Agriculture, which was to be effected by Tull and Bakewell in the eighteenth century, it will be well to call to mind what the conditions were like before they started their work.

Fig. 3 shows our home-town of Great Berkhampstead, in Hertfordshire, in the early part of the thirteenth century, and it will serve our purpose quite well, because country life in England had altered very little in the 500 years between the early thirteenth and the early eighteenth centuries. This was one of the great difficulties with which the English people had to deal when Industrialism was let loose on them—not only the thorough-going nature of the change, but the suddenness of the transition.

The three Common Fields were in the south of the town. Wheat and rye were sown in one of these, and barley, oats, peas and beans in the second, while the third was left fallow. The fields were cut up into narrow acre or half-acre strips and divided from one another by grass banks, or balks. A man would have holdings in each of the three fields, so much time was wasted in going from one field to another. The two fields which were in cultivation were fenced off from the sowing to the harvest, and then the fences were taken down and the cattle driven by the herdsman to feed off the stubble and weeds. The meadows for

FIG. 4.—The Smith.

hay were treated in the same way, cut up into strips, and fenced off between Lady Day and Midsummer Day, when the hay was cut, and after this the fences came down and the cattle grazed on the aftermath. The Waste, or Common, was for the pigs and the cattle when the fields failed and here the people went wooding to find what they could "by hook or by crook." The rams and bulls were the property of the parish, as were the cumbersome ploughs, drawn perhaps by oxen.

There were mills where the corn could be ground, and in places like Berkhampstead, markets where they could sell their butter, eggs and poultry. The exchange of commodities was a much simpler business than it is to-day, and the supply was regulated by a demand which could be estimated almost to half a pound of butter. The inns for refreshment were opposite the market place ; the church where they worshipped close by. Then there was the smith, who shod the horses and forged the ploughshares ; the wheelwright, who could make not only wheels, but the

4

waggons to go on them. The carpenter was a good tradesman, and could construct any thing in wood from a field-gate to a coffin. All these people were dependent on agriculture, and helped to build up a very healthy corporate life. The farmers themselves

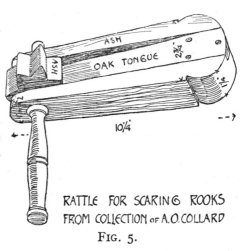

RATTLE FOR SCARING ROOKS
FROM COLLECTION of A.O.COLLARD
FIG. 5.

were very handy men and made many of their own implements—a winter's evening was well spent by the fireside in fashioning a flail for threshing. The women could spin and weave, make lace and plait straw, as well as milk the cows and bake their own bread in their brick ovens.

In fact they carried the doctrine of self-help to such extremes that they were very nearly self-supporting and independent of outside assistance. Occasionally there would be a fair in the Market Place, where pennies would be wrung out of the good man's purse for luxuries.

It was a civilization which was extremely strong and stable—it was broad-based on the land and sat securely like a pyramid, or stood erect if you will, like an oak held by its knotted roots in Wealden clay. And it was beautiful with the same unself-conscious beauty as the oak. Unfortunately they become rarer year by year, but where will you find anything more lovely than untouched English villages ? They are always in tune with Nature, and that came about very largely because the people were content to build with local materials—stone in the Cotswolds, timber framing where the oaks grew, and brick where there were good brick earths. Architecturally the church and houses may be very simple, and not at all grand, but

5

FIG. 6.—Wooden Feeding Trough.

nevertheless they are just right. If something grander is demanded then there are the cathedrals to justify Faith by works. These people were not clods—they had Faith, lived in Hope, and practised Charity.

It was very difficult for the inhabitants of such villages to change ; why should they ?—especially if, as at Berkhampstead, an old castle watched over the place to remind them of their feudal origin. What had been sufficient for their fathers was good enough for them. If a man like Tull came along and suggested that by doing this, that, or the other, they could improve matters, they remained unconvinced, and experiments were very difficult. You could not, for example, cross-plough your long, narrow strips in the Common Fields, nor delay matters for observation. At the appointed time down came the fences, and the cattle nosed their way over your ground. If the open field system of agriculture did not lend itself to experiment it yet had many points. It was based on co-operation. If it did not produce much foodstuff per acre, it kept many people usefully employed. It helped a good many lame dogs over stiles who have since got left behind. From the economical point of view it was not very much good trying to grow more food than you needed. It was difficult to exchange, because the roads were so bad that wheeled traffic was nearly impossible. Where, as in the case of Berkhampstead, the little township had been built on a road which was old when the Romans came, and some traces of the foundations they had added might be found to prevent a waggon sinking in up to its

FIG. 7.—Wooden Scoop.

6

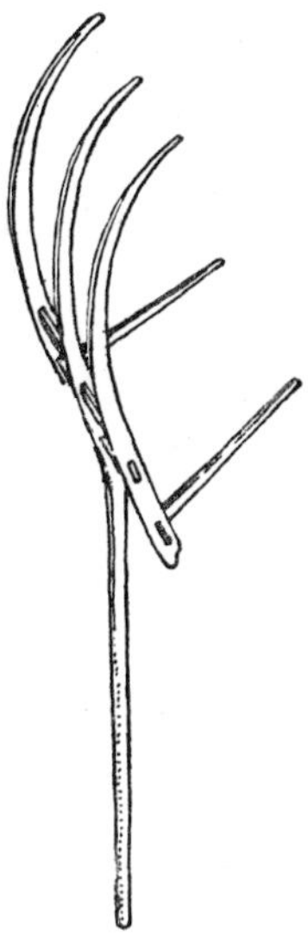

axles, movement was possible. Off the Roman roads the country lanes, which twisted and turned, began their life as the paths between the Common Fields, which led up to the Waste, and so across it, avoiding quagmire and puddles by wide detour, until the next village was reached. The pack-horse was the only possible method of transporting the scanty manufactures of the early eighteenth century. In Celia Fiennes' Diary of the seventeenth century we read of the " very deep bad roads. . . . I was near 11 hours going but 25 miles," and Celia was riding, not driving. We find the same thing in Parson Woodforde's Diary of the end of the eighteenth century. Still this did not trouble a people very much who were nearly self-supporting,

FIG. 8.—A Well-made Implement.

and, remember, there were not any great towns. Even London was only what we now call the city of London. Fig. 22 shows the Old Brompton Road, London, with fields and trees, in 1822, and Cobbett, in 1823, writes of a field of wheat at Earl's Court, set amongst the market gardens. The City of Westminster was reached by going along the Strand, where palaces stood in their own grounds running down to Thames side. The meat the cities needed walked in on foot. Turkeys from Norfolk and cattle from Kent. We noticed once when we were motoring down the Old Kent Road that dismal, vulgar-looking public-houses still retained old pleasant

FIG. 9.—A Water Cart.

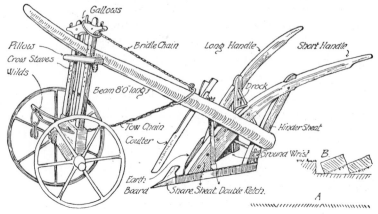

FIG. 10.—Tull's Common Two-wheeled Plough, 1733.

names as a reminder of a time when they were inns for
the refreshment of drovers bringing their cattle to Smithfield.

Another point to remember is, that before James Watt
perfected his steam engine there was no other source of
power, except a man's own muscles, or those of his horse,
or wind and water. As these were less powerful than the
steam engine, fewer people were concentrated in the early
workshops than the later factories. People could work in
their own houses, and though they may have worked long
hours, they could work to suit themselves. Celia Fiennes
tells us of the manufacture of serges at Exeter in the
seventeenth century. The yarn was made by the spinsters,
who brought it into the market, where it was bought by
the weavers, who wove it on their own looms. They sold
their cloth to the fullers, who cleaned it with fullers' earth
to remove the oil and grease. Fine flowered silks were
woven in Canterbury; crapes, calamanco and damasks in
Norwich; stockings in Nottingham, and paper in Kent;
and so it remained in the eighteenth century. There were
no hideous manufacturing districts in England, hatched in
grey as they are to-day on the A.A. maps, as places to
be avoided.

8

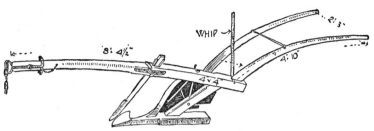

FIG. 11.—Wooden Swing Plough.

We have written of the best side of the picture of life
as lived in England in the early eighteenth century. It
makes us agree with Socrates, in Xenophon's " Œconomicus," that agriculture is the mother and nurse of the other
arts, and the best of all occupations by which men can
gain a living—that when agriculture flourishes, all the
other occupations are vigorous, but when the land lies
barren, men decay.

There was the other side of course. If we could go back
we should be shocked at many things. We should find the
people cruel, or think them so. They could see a man
hanged, and regard it as a spectacle—tell you how, when
the man was left hanging, the executioner would pull on
his legs to shorten his sufferings, and detail the length of
them. In the Woodforde Diary we find that Robert
Biggen, who had been convicted of stealing potatoes, was
whipped through the streets of Cary at a cart's tail by the
hangman. The triangular route is detailed, and sounds a
long one. Because Robert was an old offender 17s. 6d.
was collected and given to the hangman to encourage him
not to shirk the whipping. The people's surroundings and
habits cannot have been very cleanly, or they would not
have suffered from diseases engendered by filth. The
mortality was shocking—small-pox, consumption and
fevers carried off people in their prime, and only the fittest
of the babies survived. They gorged themselves like
animals, and many of them, judged by pictures, were as
gross as swine.

9

Now we come to the beginning of Industrialism, and we are going to suggest that this was really started, not by James Watt with his steam engine in 1765, but by Tull with his drill at the very beginning of the century. It was Tull who increased the food supplies—

FIG. 12.—Breast Plough from Wellingore, Lincolnshire.
(*Science Museum, London.*)

this increased the population, and without an increase in the population there would not have been any surplus to be employed in tending James Watt's engine.

Jethro Tull was born at Basildon, Berks, in 1674, and lived till 1741. He matriculated from S. John's College, Oxford, on July 7th, 1691, when he became a Law student at Gray's Inn, London, and on May 19th, 1699, was called to the Bar. Tull married on October 26th, 1699. This sounds like the early history of a Lord Chancellor, and not of the man who was to revolutionize agriculture. Here is an interesting point to note—how often revolutionary work is done in England by the amateur. The average Englishman is critical and cantankerous and does better work on his own than working in a team. The Industrial Revolution was largely the work of amateurs, kicking against the pricks of established customs and authority.

Tull's opportunity and work came about in this way. His health was poor ; in the Preface to his book he says : " tho' almost all my Life has been a continued Sickness " ; so he returned to the country from where he came and, coming back with a seeing eye, took stock of farming,

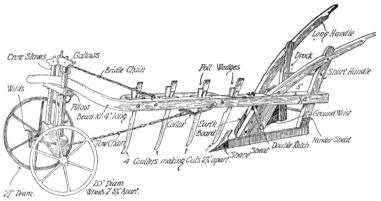

FIG. 13.—Jethro Tull's Four-coultered Plough (1733).

and found that it was still being carried on in the old-fashioned way that we have described on p. 3, and he thought that such methods must be altered.

Other people must have felt this too, because, though Tull was to meet with much opposition and receive little in the way of thanks, his ideas were found to be good, and gradually gained ground. His main idea is expressed in the title to his book, " The Horse-Hoing Husbandry : or, an Essay on the Principles of Tillage and Vegetation Wherein is shown a Method of introducing a Sort of Vineyard-Culture into the Corn-Fields, in order to Increase their Product, and diminish the common Expence ; By the Use of Instruments described in Cuts." It should be noticed that Tull places the principles of Tillage first, and these were his main contribution. The Instruments he describes come second. His book was not published till 1733. Tull seems to have started farming soon after his marriage, because he invented his first drill about 1701, and before he had seen the vineyards on his travels between 1711 and 1714.

Let us first consider the disadvantages of the old system. Sowing broadcast was very wasteful of seed. Tull says, " It was very difficult to find a Man that could sow Clover tolerably ; they had a Habit (from which they

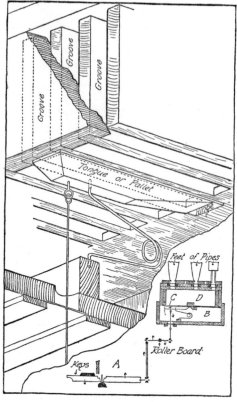

FIG. 14.—The Tongue or Pallet of the Organ.

could not be driven) to throw it once with the Hand to two large Strides, and go twice on each Cast; thus with nine or ten Pound of seed to an Acre, two-thirds of the Ground was unplanted, and on the rest 'twas so thick that it did not prosper." (See Cobbett's remarks on this on p. 118.) So Tull made his first drill, which did the same work with two pounds of seed. He also used his drill as early as 1701 for wheat, making the channels at 1 foot distance at a cost of 6d. the acre, using only one bushel of seed to the acre. Now here were facts which could not be overlooked by Tull's neighbours—he not only saved seed, but by sowing it in drills, or lines, the weeds could be kept down by hoeing, and the ground cultivated and kept friable in a far more economical way than was possible when the field was covered with crops coming up just anyhow. This must be kept in mind, that Tull not only invented his drill, but initiated good cultivation. Tull suffered the common fate of innovators; his book hints at it. He expected acclamation, but received only grumbles. The farmer is the most conservative of men, and probably

Tull's neighbours complained amongst themselves of this lawyer, of all persons, who was drilling seed with a machine. Why could not the man be satisfied with the ways of his father ?—and so on, and so forth—but the man Tull went on and must be reckoned as one of the makers of modern England.

But we are running on a little too quickly. We will follow Tull's example and start with the plough, or plow as he calls it, as Fig. 10. He shows first the common two-wheeled plough used in Berkshire, Hampshire, Oxfordshire, and Wiltshire, and most other counties of south Britain, except where there were miry clays to clog the wheels. In heavy land the swing plough with a more horizontal beam and no wheels was used, as Fig. 11. It is interesting to note that a wheeled plough is shown in the Norman Bayeux Tapestry, and a swing plough in the fourteenth-century Luttrell Psalter.

The function of a plough is to break up land that has been under grass, or lying fallow, and it works in this way. If we refer to Fig. 10, which is Tull's common plough, the coulter makes the vertical cut, and the share the horizontal one. The depth of the furrow, about 7 inches, is regulated by raising or lowering the beam on its pillow ; with a swing plough the ploughman does this by raising up, or bearing down on, the plough handles. The furrow slice is turned over by the earth-board. In the ordinary way a ploughman does not plough up and down the field with the furrows side by side, but moves across the headland by the hedge, until the furrow slices lie in the direction of A, Fig. 10. Where the slices incline towards one another is the ridge, and where they go from one another is the water furrow used for drainage. The distance between these furrows depends on the character of the soil, and its need for drainage.

Now one of the difficulties with which the farmer has to contend is how to get rid of the grass and weeds. B, Fig. 10, shows the furrow slices upside down after ploughing,

13

and if the weather is favourable to them the weeds will soon grow up again between the slices.

Tull points out that "another way to conquer a strong turf, is, to plough it first with a Breast-Plow, very thin," as Fig. 12, but this was a very expensive proceeding. In the later plough, Fig. 85, there is an ingenious little share in front of the coulter, which skimmed off the weeds and turned them over to be buried under the furrow slice by the action of the earth-board.

It was to remedy this that Tull invented his four-coultered plow, as Fig. 13. You can think of the indignation of his fellow farmers, and almost hear them saying, " Whoever heard of a four-coultered plough ? " The beam had to be made longer to accommodate the three additional coulters, and these were placed, each of them, $2\frac{1}{2}$ inches to the right of the one behind, and the points of the three in front were kept up somewhat higher than the one behind in front of the share. This made the vertical cut, which cut off the furrow slice 10 inches wide, but when this had been severed by the share and turned over by the earth-board the slice had three vertical cuts in it made by the other coulters, so that the roots of the grass and weeds were more easily dried and destroyed and the ground made more friable. We have put Tull's interesting old names for the various parts of the plough on the drawings.

JETHRO TULL'S DRILL.—The land having been pre-pared by ploughing and harrowing, we can pass on to the drilling which followed, and was made possible by Tull's great invention ; and it was great and vital because it dealt with the food of man. It seems to us so simple an idea that it is hardly worth talking about, but then most great inventions are simple, and have to be if they are to be useful—the merit comes in having the idea.

The function of Tull's drill was to make the channels, sow the seed, and cover the rows all in one operation.

The principal parts of the drill were the seed-box, hopper, plough and harrow. Tull says, " Of these the

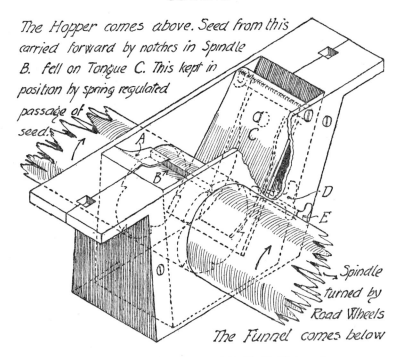

The Hopper comes above. Seed from this carried forward by notches in Spindle B. fell on Tongue C. This kept in position by spring regulated passage of seed.

A B C D E

Spindle turned by Road Wheels

The Funnel comes below

FIG. 15.—The Seed Box of Tull's Drill (1733).

Seed-Box is the chief; it measures (or rather numbers) out the Seed which it receives from the Hopper: It is for this Purpose as an artificial Hand, which performs the Task of delivering out the Seed, more equally than can be done by a natural Hand." We will start then with the seed-box, and here Tull is of the greatest interest, because he tells us just how he went to work in designing his drill. Some of the boys and girls who read this book may have ambitions in the way of inventing things, and yet doubt their ability in this direction. Tull will give them comfort —great ideas do not spring from the head, fully armed, like Athene from the brow of Zeus. Happy accident plays a great part in invention, and the ability to see that adaptation may be useful.

Tull was confronted with this problem of the seed-box which was to take the place of the hand, and then he thought of what he calls the tongue (and modern organ builders call the pallet) in the sound-board of an organ. He had learned to play the organ when he was young, and must have taken it to pieces, one hopes with the consent of his parents, because he seems to have thoroughly understood its mechanism. We have reconstructed this, with the assistance of an old friend, F. Pickering Walker, in Fig. 14. Odd information is sometimes very useful, and there may be some more ideas for inventors in the organ. In the smaller diagram A shows how when the playing end of the key is depressed the other rises, because the key is pivoted on its centre, and how by a series of rods the tongue at C is opened and lets the compressed air, provided by the bellows from a continuous chamber at B, into a series of grooves or mortices at D, on the top of which come the feet of the pipes. There is a groove for each key on the keyboard, each with its own tongue, and the grooves vary in width to suit the sizes of the pipes. But Tull points out that the tongue shuts flat against the surface of the groove and is kept in position by the spring shown. This was practical for measuring out the air to be let into the pipes, but clearly you could not measure out wheat in this way, because it would get jammed in between the tongue and its seating.

Tull's next step was to design his seed-box, as Fig. 15, in brass, in two halves, which were bolted together and made wider at the bottom than the top to prevent what Tull calls the " arching " or jamming of the seed in the box.

Fig. 16 shows the drill itself, which made channels for a treble row of wheat at 7-inch partitions.

We can now give Tull's summing up of his inventions : " The first Idea that I form'd of this Machine, was thus ; I imagin'd the Mortise, or Groove, brought from the Sound-Board of an Organ, together with the Tongue and Spring, all of them much alter'd ; the Mortise having a Hole therein, and put on upon one of the iron Gudgeons of the Wheel-Barrow, which Gudgeon being enlarg'd to an

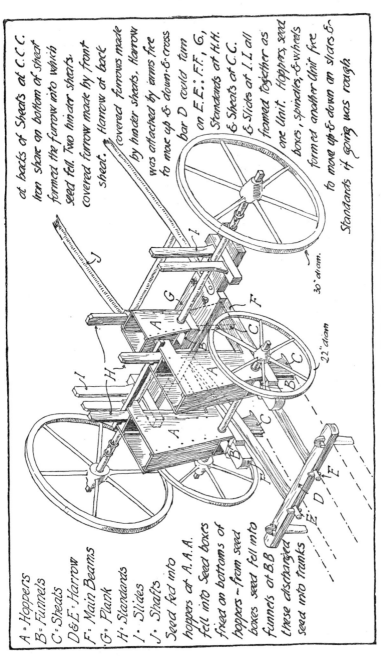

A = Hoppers
B = Funnels
C = Sheats
D & E = Harrow
F = Main Beams
G = Plank
H = Standards
I = Slides
J = Shafts

Seed fed into hoppers at A.A.A. fell into Seed boxes fixed on bottoms of hoppers – from seed boxes seed fell into funnels at B.B these discharged seed into franks

at backs of Sheats at C.C.C. Iron share on bottom of sheat formed the furrow into which seed fell. Two hinder shafts covered furrow made by front sheat. Harrow at back covered furrows made by hinder sheats. Harrow was attached by arms fre to mov up & down & cross bar D could turn on E.E.: F.F., G, Standards at H.H. & Sheats at C.C. & Slides at I.I. all framed together as one Unit. Hoppers seed boxes, spindles, & wheels formed another Unit fre to mov up & down on slars & Standards if going was rough

30" diam.

22" diam.

FIG. 16.—Jethro Tull's Seed Drill (1733).

Inch and a Half diameter, having on it the Notches of the Cylinder of a Cyder-Mill, on that Part of it which should be within the Mortise, and this Mortise made in the Ear of the Wheel-Barrow (thro' which the Gudgeon usually passes) made broad enough for the Purpose; this I hoped, for any thing I saw to the contrary, might perform this Work of Drilling, and herein I was not deceived."

Tull goes on to say that placing a box over the mortise to carry the seed was so obvious as to occasion little thought; nor placing the spindle on two wheels, one at each end, instead of on one as the wheelbarrow, or contriving the plough to make the channels. At first the channels were left open and the seed covered by a harrow; then this was added to the drill and the whole done in one operation.

And that, we think, is all that need be said about Tull's drill, and we have written what we have to say at considerably less length than the designer. In the 1733 edition of Tull's book he gives 12,662 words to describing the seed-box alone before he starts on the rest of the machine, and it is heavy reading, but very well worth the time and trouble.

After all it was a great achievement to take parts of an organ, wheelbarrow and cyder-mill and so alter and adapt them that it was possible to invent one of the most useful implements of agriculture. There is hope for us all in this direction. Tull saw to the root of the matter when he wrote: "Some waste their whole Lives in studying how to arm Death with New Engines of Horror, and inventing an Infinite Variety of Slaughter; but think it beneath Men of Learning (who only are capable of doing it) to employ their learned Labours in the Invention of New (or even improving the Old) Instruments for increasing of Bread."

These remarks of Tull apply to the invention of tanks in the war of 1914–18. "These engines of horror" were designed by clapping a fighting turret on to an agricultural Holt caterpillar tractor.

Fig. 16a.—Lively Activity on an Eighteenth-Century Farm.

From an anonymous coloured engraving.

Fig. 16b.—A familiar and welcome country figure : the Pedlar and his pack, mounted and on foot.

Aquatints by W. H. Pyne, ca. 1800.

William Cobbett, of whom we shall have more to say presently, gave Tull the credit for inventing the the first drill. If the effect of this was the "increasing of bread," then an increasing of the population followed as a natural result, so Tull can be counted as one of the makers of Modern England. When men were hunters in the Old Stone Age the factor which decided the number of the hunters was the area which was necessary to support and feed the animals which they hunted. In the New Stone Age men caught the animals and tended them as herdsmen, and began to grow crops to feed both the animals and themselves, and in this way the land could support a larger population. The extraordinary thing is that from the time of the New Stone Age up to Tull there was not any very real or essential change.

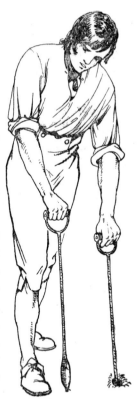

FIG. 17.—Dibbling.

The system of farming which is described on p. 3 was really very primitive; just sufficient was grown to keep the people alive, and there was very little margin. The population could not increase because there was no great margin of food left over. When the winter came there was only hay to feed the cattle on, so many of them were killed and salted down—there was no possibility of increasing the flocks and herds. If a bad summer came and the hay failed, then the herds starved. It was this fact which made the landowners so keen on the Game Laws; they were pot-hunters and chased the wild deer and hare, and shot the pheasant and partridge, because it gave them fresh meat in the winter and made a change from salted meat. It was an explanation of the large pigeon cots

C
19

which can still be found ; a plump pigeon in a pie was prettier eating than pickled pork. It explains as well why " Peter Piper picked a peck of pickled pepper "—it was to try and make the pickled pork palatable.

THE TURNIP.—All of which leads us to the turnip ; and here Tull did good work, because he invented a special turnip drill. He says in his book, " As far as I can be inform'd, 'tis but of late Years that Turneps have been introduc'd as an Improvement in the Field." Again, " The greatest Turnep-Improvement used by the Farmer is for his Cattle in the Winter."

The turnip of course was known as a garden vegetable long before this. It may be that a flock of sheep, cropping the scanty herbage of a winter field, raided a farmer's garden, as once occurred to us, and ate off all the turnips. If this happened the farmer may well have thought : Why not grow the turnips on a large scale in a field, and then let the sheep eat them there, and to regulate their eating and not let them spoil the whole field we will move them along in enclosures made by hurdles. This was first done in Suffolk about 1724. It sounds so simple, yet nobody had thought of it before. Yet though it sounds simple it was destined to be revolutionary. Other stock could be fed on turnips, so that it meant not only more meat, but more milk and butter, and, what was just as important, more manure. Tull had already by 1724 shown the farmers how to grow more corn ; more corn meant more straw ; the straw could be placed in the yards and there turned into manure, which would not only improve impoverished old soils but enable new light ones to be brought into cultivation.

Again, it is usual to state that enclosures were necessary to meet the demand for food from an increasing industrial population ; but there would not have been an industrial population except for Tull.

We shall have something to say about the Enclosure Acts presently, but here we may remind boys and girls that enclosing the land did not reclaim it— planting quick-set hedges does not make corn grow. The enclosures followed as a natural result of the work of Tull.

A) ESSEX SICKLE LAST USED BY MR TYRELL OF BOCKING IN 1873. TEETH HAVE BEEN WORN AWAY. B) 60 YEARS OLD BUT UNUSED & SHOWS TEETH. STILL MADE BY THOS. STANIFORTH OF SHEFFIELD FOR USE IN SCOTTISH HIGHLANDS & EXPORT TO PRIMITIVE PEOPLES. TANG IS NOT CRANKED BUT BLADE & HANDLE ARE ON THE SAME LINE.

INCHES

FIG. 18.—Sickles given to the Authors by Alfred Hills of Braintree.

Charles Townshend, the second viscount (1674–1738), is another great name. Townshend was an enthusiast who carried on agricultural experiments at Raynham, Norfolk, 1730. He was called "Turnip" Townshend by the wits, who, because they were turnip-headed themselves, were amused by his enthusiasms. Pope tells us that a favourite subject of his conversation was "that kind of rural improvement which arises from turnips."

Townshend is as well credited with the introduction of the Norfolk, or Four Course, system of cultivation. The fields were cropped in the following rotation. First came wheat or oats sown in the winter; the next year oats or barley, sown in the spring. The third year clover, rye, vetches, swedes and kale for winter feed, and the fourth year turnips. The sheep were then hurdled over the turnips, and manured the ground so that it was ready for wheat the next year.

This four-course system has lasted until to-day, when the land is being put down to grass and the wise farmer grows meat, milk and poultry.

The next great name to be mentioned is that of Bakewell, a farmer of Dishley, near Loughborough, in Leicestershire, who was born in 1725. He devoted his attention to the improvement of cattle. Before his time they had been leggy beasts, who wandered about over the common fields after harvest or were taken on to the waste to pick up a living as best they could. The sheep were more valued for their golden fleece than the mutton they produced. Bakewell started his experiments about 1745, and by carefully selecting the animals from which he bred produced far more meat per animal than had been done before. Tull had already produced the bread, and when Bakewell added the meat times were ripe for the increase in the population which was to produce the Industrial Revolution, as well as manufactured goods for the Empire overseas.

Another great name in agriculture is Thomas Coke of Holkham. He came into his estate in 1776, and there carried on the experiments which were to raise his rent roll from £2200 in 1776 to £20,000 in 1816. He carried on the good work of Townshend, and worked on the principle that " No fodder, no beasts ; no beasts, no manure ; no manure, no crop."

Coke must have been a very pleasant man. It was in 1778 that he started the meetings of farmers at his home which were held annually afterwards and became known as the Holkham meetings. They were held in the great house which had been built by Coke's ancestor, Lord Leicester. This house was started about 1734 and was a quarter of a century in building, and seems to have been inspired by Lord Leicester and his friend, Lord Burlington, with professional assistance from Kent, but was carried out by a Norwich architect, Matthew Brettingham. It is shown on D, Fig. 33.

Though not built by Coke himself, Holkham well illustrates a great eighteenth-century house, and the eighteenth was the century for great houses. The chart on p. xiv gives the dates of some of these, and in many cases they now remain as an embarrassment to their owners in these

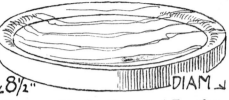

FIG. 19.—Wooden (Sycamore) Trencher.

harder days. When they were built, however, they were centres of life centred on the land. The Holkham gatherings lasted for a week, and were attended by hundreds of people from all over the world. Agriculture was recognized as the mother of all the crafts and a matter of interest to all ; where an aristocrat like Coke was a good man and a leader of the people, he needed a large house to entertain his friends.

Cobbett spoke well of him in his " Rural Rides," when he says that " expressions made use of towards him that affectionate children use towards the best of parents."

Arthur Young is another great name in eighteenth-century agriculture. Born in 1741, he became Secretary of the Board of Agriculture in 1793, and died in 1820. He was an enthusiastic advocate for enclosing the common fields and adopting Tullian methods of tillage.

Prof. S. E. Morison, writing in *The Times* on February 22nd, 1932, 200 years after the birth of George Washington, said of him, " Washington's greatest teacher and deepest love was the land." He was one of Arthur Young's correspondents, and in one of his letters wrote, " How much more delightful is the task of making improvements on the earth than all the vain glory which can be acquired from ravaging it by the most uninterrupted career of conquests." And again, " To see plants rise from the earth and flourish by the superior skill and bounty of the labourer fills a contemplative mind with ideas which are more easy to be conceived than expressed." When Washington went to Mount Vernon in 1759 he found that his estate was in bad order and devoted himself to putting things right.

He became an eager student of Tull's Horse-Hoing Husbandry, Horne's " Gentleman Farmer," and Weston's New System of Agriculture, with fox-hunting as his recreation. Perhaps because of this training he was able to do his other work so well.

This is hardly the place to discuss the technical details of the Land Enclosure Acts, but briefly the principle was to gather the land together in larger holdings on which Tullian methods could be carried out. Without the Enclosures the people would have starved during the Napoleonic Wars. The bad part of the Enclosures was that the smaller men became dispossessed of any holding, and so had no stake in the land. They became labourers, and their position was very bad indeed, as we shall see when we get to the beginning of the nineteenth century.

THE WOODFORDE DIARY.—Having dealt with the great men and shown how their fortunes were affected by the times, we can now turn to humbler folk, and here we have been helped by the wonderful diary of a country parson. This deals with the life of the Rev. James Woodforde, who was born in 1740 and died in 1803. So the diarist, in the short span of his life, saw the end of the Old Merry England and the foundations laid of the Empire and Modern Industrial England. The Diary was edited by Mr. John Beresford, and published by the Oxford University Press, and we should like to thank them here for their permission to make use of the information contained in it.

So far as we are concerned the great interest to us in the Diary begins when Woodforde is presented to the College Living of Weston, in Norfolk, in 1774. This was supposed to be worth £300 per annum. As Woodforde was able to lead a very pleasant life at Weston and keep two maids, a footman, a house boy and a farm hand, it shows that money was worth at least four times more then than it is now.

AGRICULTURE.—It must be remembered that Wood-forde was not only a parson—and a very good one—caring for the souls of his parishioners, but a practical farmer, farming his own glebe. When the farmers who paid him tithe came to the tithe frolics we may be sure that he and they had very much in common and, like Townshend, could discuss "that kind of rural improvement which arises from turnips."

He was assisted in his farming by the faithful Benjamin Legate, whom he engaged in September, 1776, as farm hand at £10 per annum—Ben living at the parsonage house. He was assisted by one of the maids, who did the milking, and the footman and boy helped on occasions.

Women were paid 6d. a day for weeding, plus 1½d. extra for beer; a man for ditching got 10d. a rod of 16½ feet.

The land was ploughed in October with a plough of the type of Fig. 10, and after it had been harrowed and rolled the wheat was set in November. Now here comes a very interesting detail. One would have imagined that, after Tull, his drill would have come into general use, but this was not the case in East Anglia; the seed was often set by hand. Arthur Young, later on, was in the course of his journeys to find that wheat was still sown broadcast, dibbled and set by hand, and sown by a drill. It takes a tremendous time in England for new ideas to filter through.

There is an entry in the Woodforde Diary that they "Finished setting 3½ acres of Wheat this even. The Quantity of seed Wheat to set the whole was 6 bushels 1 peck, that is, as near as can be 7½ pecks to the Acre. Expence of setting it 8s. per acre, allowance, etc., included —I had 4 dibblers and 16 setters and they finished the whole in 2 days."

From "Sketches of Rural Affairs" (1851) we find that dibbling was extensively practised in Suffolk, Norfolk and the lighter lands of Essex. "The soil being duly prepared for the crop a light roller is passed over it. A man then walks backwards with an iron dibble in each hand with which he strikes two rows of holes in each sod, and he is followed by children, who drop a few grains in each hole. The seed is covered in by a bush harrow and sometimes by a roller," as Fig. 17.

To dibble a hole to set a plant or seed in must be nearly as old as the hills. Its application to setting wheat was first advocated by Sir Hugh Plat in 1600, in his book on " The Setting of Corne." Plat traces the idea to a " silly wench " who, when dibbling some other seed, accidentally dropped some wheat in one of the holes. This did so much better than the broadcast-sown corn that some adopted the idea.

Woodforde's dibbling was fairly successful; he tells us that he measured a stalk of wheat from a field that was formerly a furze cover, and it measured 6 feet 7 inches and about a barley corn, and when harvested weighed 4 stone 9 lb. to the bushel.

Going through the year we find that turnips were sold for 30s. an acre, and these were to be fed off by sheep, not pulled, by old Lady Day.

The point of this was that, though the owner of the sheep got feed for them when it was scarce, the land was well manured for the following corn crop.

So we come to the harvest in August. The oats were cut in the morning before the dew was off them. It was cut with a sickle having the form of a reap-hook, with an edge like a saw, as Fig. 18. You often see sickles drawn which are not all sickle shaped. Fig. 18 has been made from a full-sized tracing made from the blades of old ones, so it should be correct. The Norfolk custom was to give the reapers a good breakfast; at eleven o'clock plum cakes with caraway seeds in them, and liquor to drink; a good dinner with plum puddings and beer again at four. So they did not do so badly.

In September it was usual for the harvesters to call upon the principal inhabitants, and each set was given 1s.—as a harvest thanksgiving one supposes. When one lived as close to the ground as the eighteenth-century

FIG. 20.—A Dog Turnspit in an Inn Kitchen at Newcastle Emlyn, South Wales.

By Thomas Rowlandson, about 1800.

FIG. 21.—A Farm Kitchen and Bakehouse, about 1800.

FIG. 22.—The Suburbs : Old Brompton Road in 1822.

By G. Scharf.

people did a good harvest was a matter for general thanksgiving and happiness.

The corn went into the barn and was threshed out on the threshing floor just inside the doors. It was not put up into stacks until threshing machines were invented which could be taken to the stacks. Fig. 92, Vol. II. "Everyday Things," shows the details of the flail used in threshing.

After the harvest the farmers settled their accounts, and in a small village it is quite easy to see that the basis of trade is the exchange of commodities, and money only the medium by which this is done. Farmer, miller, carpenter, smith, butcher, and so on, paid their bills with a few guinea pieces and some small change. The farmer let the carpenter have some wheat, which he sent to the miller to grind, but as he had done work for both of them it did not take them very long to settle up.

When the farmers paid their tithes to the parson early in December, they did so at a party or frolic, as it was called in Norfolk, held in the Parsonage. It was really a very good feed of roast beef and boiled mutton, with plenty of plum puddings, with wine, punch and ale to drink.

The Woodforde Diary helps us as to the rent of land. When Woodforde leaves Ansford for Weston he lets 30 acres in Somerset to a farmer for seven years at no less than £35 per annum, tenant paying all taxes except Land Tax.

Again, 15 acres of charity land was let at £16 5s. In 1801 an estate of about 100 acres near Chichester, in Sussex, was sold for £3500.

FOOD.—Woodforde had not been long at Weston before he was invited to join the "Rotation Clubb," for dining at one another's houses on Mondays. This brings up the subject of food, which plays such a large part in the Diary. Here is the first Rotation dinner which Woodforde gave when his turn came on January 20th, 1777 : " A couple of Rabbits smothered with onions, a Neck of Mutton boiled and a Goose roasted with a Currant Pudding and a plain one. They drank Tea in the afternoon, played a pool of Quadrille after, drank a glass or two of Punch, and went away about 8 o'clock." One rule was that the Club did not add a supper or give any vails (tips) to servants. This was an important detail, because tipping was very general in the eighteenth century.

Breakfast seems to have been a lighter meal—oysters and tea and bread and butter, or cold tongue instead of oysters. Elevens at noon was in the nature of a snack. Dinners at two to three were heavy, and followed by tea-drinking, with cake perhaps, but supper about nine was quite substantial enough to be regarded as another dinner. The food was all good and wholesome, though once Woodforde complains of heartburn after eating pike with a sauce compounded of anchovy sauce, walnut pickle and melted butter. Again he has a bad night after roasted lobster for supper. He ate Parmezan cheese in 1779 for the first time, and liked it.

They ate all the coarse fish. Tench is a favourite dish, as is pike, stuffed with a " pudding in its belly."

They were enormous meat eaters. For example, on December 7th, 1790, Woodforde pays £46 5s. for a year's meat, and in the same period spends £22 18s. 6d. for malt, and only £5 7s. 6d. for 48 stone of flour. He may of course have provided the miller with his own wheat. As breast of veal and pork was $3\frac{1}{2}d.$ per lb. and hind quarter of lamb and turkey $4\frac{1}{2}d.$ per lb., turbot 6d. per lb., salmon 7d., and a pair of soles weighing 1 lb. cost 3d., oysters 8d. per score, we can see the quantities of food which were consumed. There can be no doubt that far more people died of over-eating in the eighteenth century than starvation ; they were continually taking rhubarb and vomits.

People brewed their own beer, and for 36 gallons allowed 1 coomb (4 bushels or $\frac{1}{2}$ quarter) of malt and $1\frac{1}{2}$ lb. of hops.

The large houses could brew eight barrels at a time.

Mead was another home-made drink. 14 lb. of honey were put into 4 gallons of water, with ginger and two handfuls of dried elder flowers, and boiled for more than an hour, and skimmed meanwhile. It was then poured into a tub to cool, and a large gravy spoon of fresh yeast added when almost cold, and kept in a

FIG. 23.—A Turnspit.

warm place at night. The mead was drawn off next day and put into a barrel. We have made mead from this recipe, and excellent stuff it is, with, curiously enough, a slightly beery flavour.

The tea was bought from a smuggler, and even then cost 9s. and 10s. 6d. a pound. From the same source a tub of gin (19 bottles and 1 pint) cost £1 6s., and half an anchor of rum £1 15s.

It is misleading to judge the drinking habits of the eighteenth century by our own time. Woodforde's niece Nancy came to live with him, and a very nice person she was. She had a bad knee, and her doctor prescribed at least a pint of port wine a day ; to be on the right side she drinks " between a Pint and a Quart "—say 1½ pints—as medicine ! The effects, however, were so marked and so unhappy, that fortunately she soon abandoned the treatment.

All the eighteenth-century table appointments were very beautiful ; the china, stoneware and silver have never been bettered, but these must have been kept for the parties. In the *Lonsdale Magazine*, 1822, we find that " the richer sort of people had a service of pewter, but amongst the middling and poorer classes the dinner was eaten off wooden trenchers," as Fig. 19, turned out of sycamore.

D*

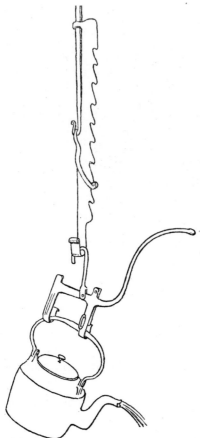

FIG. 24.—Idle Back.

While we are dealing with food we will return to the question of the vails, or tips, which were not allowed at the dinners of the Rotation Club. Tips must have made a substantial addition to eighteenth-century wages —you tipped after a dinner-party and on every other possible occasion. The wages seem very low until you remember the value of the money. A maid got £5 a year, and perhaps picked up as much more ; it was really the equivalent of £40 a year to-day. A charwoman was 6d. a day.

Cooking.—Food leads us naturally to cooking, and there were no very great developments in the eighteenth century. In a country parsonage they probably cooked their food in much the same way as shown in Fig. 20, from the original by Rowlandson. This is interesting, as it shows a dog as the power for turning the spit. In other turnspits the power was supplied by a weight which had to be wound up. We illustrated a beautiful specimen of this type in Fig. 65, Vol. II. Perhaps the house boy was sometimes called the skip-jack because he had to skip to this type of jack to wind it up.

The meat was roasted in front of the fire and basted as it turned round on the spit, and the fat which dripped out of it into the pan under was called dripping. Fig. 23 shows a very simple arrangement where the spit was turned by a boy. Now we come to a pretty problem. In 1787 Woodforde had two stoves put up in his kitchen. Were these the new-fangled kitchen ranges which we discuss on p. 181 ? We rather doubt it ourselves, and think the ranges were for the smaller houses

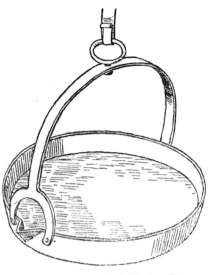

FIG. 25.—Suspended Frying Pan.

which were beginning to be built in the industrial towns. In the country the old open fire and roasting continued for a long time.

Over the fire hung a great kettle on an adjustable hanger to supply hot water, because of course there was no boiler, or any tap over the kitchen sink. The kettle was fitted with an ingenious little contrivance by which it could be tipped to pour out boiling water, as Fig. 24. A caldron could be suspended in the same way for boiling meat or making porridge, or a frying pan, as Fig. 25.

Papin's Digesters may have continued in use. John Evelyn the diarist mentions how, on April 12th, 1682, he went to a supper with several members of the Royal Society where all the food, both fish and flesh, had been cooked in a digester with less than 8 oz. of coal. The digester was really a large saucepan with an air-tight lid fitted with a safety valve. Evelyn says that the hardest bones were made as soft as cheese, that the food was delicious, and that " this philosophical supper caused mirth amongst us." Of course all the pots and pans which were used over a coal fire got filthily black and dirty.

The eighteenth-century baking was done in the brick oven. This came on the side of the open fire, so that the smoke from the oven when it was lighted could escape up the main chimney (Fig. 21).

The oven itself was circular in plan, and domed over in brick. A bundle of faggots was put inside the oven and lighted with hot ashes. When these had burned themselves out the hot ashes were raked on one side, and into the oven went the bread and all the pies and cakes, and the entrance was closed by an iron door and, as there was no chimney from the oven, or escape for the imprisoned heat, except through this doorway, the cooking was done. It was really exactly the same principle as the cooking hole outside the huts in the New Stone Age, where, after the fire had burnt itself out, the food was cooked by turves heaped over the hole. It may of course be just so much antique imagination, but one of the authors spent a con- siderable time in a farm-house in Kent when young, and in this way learned to love the land and farmers and all their doings. The loaves there were made of home-grown wheat ground into flour in the local windmill ; their shape was that of large buns ; the colour of the bread greyish ; its texture close and smell most appetizing, and it possessed remarkable staying powers. Whether any other ovens were used besides the large brick ovens we cannot say. Camp ovens as Fig. 26 were advertised for sale by the Carron Co., of Falkirk, in 1782, and they tell us that they still sell these ovens for use in the country places in Ireland, Australia and New Zealand. Made of cast iron, their sizes vary from 6 to 24 inches in diameter, and they are provided with a cover like a saucepan lid. Pushed into the glowing ashes of an open fire on their short feet, they can be used for baking, frying, stewing or boiling. It would be excellent practice for the juvenile members of a family living in the country to invest in a camp oven, build a camp round

it and see if they
could bake, fry, stew
and boil, all in this
wonderful imple-
ment. If the eggs
and bacon carried
on into the stew
what matter ? It
would be sooner than
later—that is all.

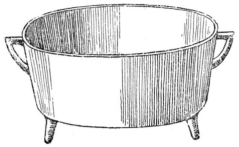

FIG. 26.—A Camp Oven.

The girdle, as Fig. 27, was suspended over the
fire, and on it the cakes, made of a batter of buttermilk and flour, were cooked—anyone who has eaten
these all hot, and split with a pat of dairy butter
inside, will agree that they are very good eating indeed ;
and these we once ate in a Welsh farm in prodigious
quantities.

There is another interesting cooking note in the Woodforde Diary. Niece Nancy had been making jam, and
complained of giddiness after. Woodforde thought she
was " too long at the stove where charcoal was burning
tho' the outward Door was open all the time." This meant
the kitchen door, because the stove was probably no more
than a raised brick hearth on which charcoal fires could
be made, and saucepans used over them on tripod stands.
Such a raised hearth can be seen in the old kitchen at
Hampton Court. Remember, a saucepan started life as a
small deep pan with a handle, in which sauces could be
made. When Nancy made red-currant jelly she used 4 lb.
of currants and 4 lb. of best lump sugar, which cost 1s. 2d
per lb. She made as well cakes, tarts, custards and jellies
when they had parties. The plum puddings served at
Tithe frolics were made of 1 lb. of sun raisins, 1 lb. of suet,
1 lb. of flour and two eggs.

Then all the washing was done at home, and they
washed every five weeks. If they changed their clothes
as frequently as we do they must have had a tremendous

FIG. 27.—The Girdle.

amount to wash, but we don't think they did. There is an amusing note in Boswell's Life of Johnson. Johnson was talking with Dr. Burney about a poor mad poet, one of whose failings was that he did not love clean linen, and then Johnson added, " I have no passion for it." However that may be, there was enough in the Wood-forde household to em-ploy two washerwomen for two days, who were paid 6d. a day each, plus breakfast and dinner ; the ironing, done by the maids, took another two days.

When the chimneys wanted sweeping the chimney sweep came with his boy, who climbed up the flue, brush in hand. Woodforde wrote that when his sweep, Holland, came to him, " he had a new Boy with him who had likely to have lost his Life this Morning at Weston House in sticking in one of their chimneys. I gave the poor boy a shilling." It seems extraordinary that such things could happen. In the nineteenth century, when brushes were introduced, the sweeps who used the new brooms called themselves Mechanical Chimney Sweeps.

As well as cooking and washing the butter had to be made. The milk was brought in and poured out into large pans and scalded over a copper (Fig. 21), and then placed in the dairy to cool. The cream was skimmed by a flat skimmer and came off in thick golden folds. For a minute it was held while the milk drained away through holes in the skimmer, and then the cream went into a crock, and the skim milk into the swill-tub for the pigs. The cream went into the churn. Fig. 28 shows one of 1 h.p., but

34

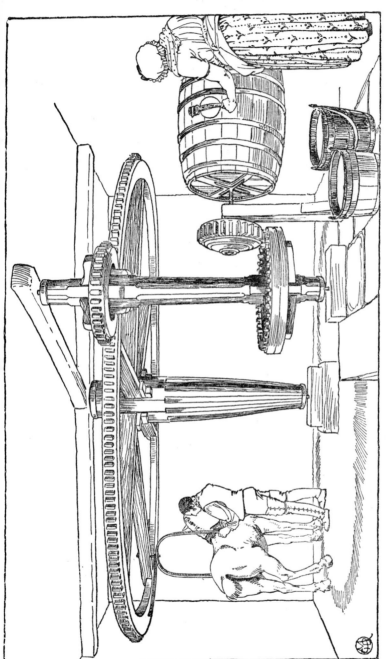

FIG. 28.—1-h.p. Churn formerly at Broughton Manor Farm, near Brierton, Bucks, now in the Science Museum, London.

6¾ DIAM.→
X 9"HIGH.

FIG. 29.—A Wooden Measure.

generally the farmer's wife supplied the power which turned the handle. The churns were either of plunger or barrel type, mounted on a stand, and inside the barrel long blades beat the cream into butter. Sometimes it took a long time for the butter to come, but when it did and the churn was opened the butter was found like granulated crumbs in the buttermilk. The butter was taken out and washed, and smacked with pats to give it shape in the kitchen sink (Fig. 21), which was a very large one made of stone, and instead of water taps there was a pump, and you plied the handle good and hard to pump up the water you wanted to wash the butter, and you used platters and bowls and pats and moulds to give it shape, all made of wood. In fact, most of your utensils were made of wood or earthenware, because enamelled iron had not been invented. Fig. 29 shows an interesting wooden measure. In Norfolk the butter was sold by the pint and not the pound.

Skim milk introduces pigs and pig killing. Pigs mean pork, bacon, sausages and oddments which are all edible. For example, souse was pickled pigs' feet and ears, and black puddings are as old as the hills. The goats' bellies filled with fat and blood mentioned in the "Odyssey" were black puddings.

We have mentioned all these things because we wanted to make the point that it was very necessary for the eighteenth-century woman to know her job. Almost everything was done within the home, and little help came from outside. Woodforde of course was fortunately placed; he was a bachelor, and lone men have an uncanny knack of finding devoted women who will work their fingers to the bone for them; and as there were very few, if any, labour-saving appliances it did mean hard work, but it did provide work to do. Take lighting for one example; to-day we enter a room and by turning on a switch light up the room at once. In the eighteenth century they only had candles, and this meant cleaning candlesticks and using snuffers to keep the wicks in order while the candles were burning, and they guttered in draught, so that the candle-

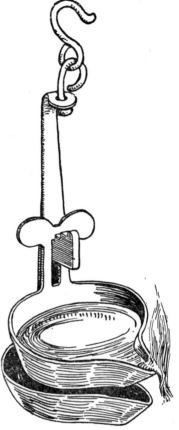

FIG. 30.—Scottish Cruzie.

sticks had to be cleaned. Though the light was soft and beautiful, you wanted many candles to make a good light. Primitive oil lamps as Fig. 30 were used.

We should like to close this chapter with a strong recommendation to our readers to read the Woodforde Diary for themselves. There are five volumes, but after a little this will only be a cause for regret. We know of no other books which give so true a picture of eighteenth-century everyday life in the country. There are many other diaries, some gossipy, others scandalous; some political, and others military; but there is only one Woodforde.

There is not only the life in the village, but its government by squire and parson ; a thing the Radicals used to shudder at, but now that it is going others may be found to regret this. You must have some form of government ; either a council, or a Soviet if you will, and these will have to be very good indeed to be better than the mild autocracy practiced by Custance, the Squire of Weston. He evidently belonged to that class of whom Cobbett wrote (p. 114) " as the resident native gentry attached to the soil and knowing the people." If the squires enjoyed the privileges of their position, they accepted their responsibilities as well and played Providence in an amiable fashion.

A conversation piece in silhouette.

FIGS. 30A, 30B.—A Fishmonger's and a Butcher's Shop.

Coloured engravings by James Pollard.

FIG. 31.
The Waggon, *c.* 1800.
By W. H. Pyne.

FIG. 32.
A London Mail and a
Stage Coach on the
Brighton Road, *c.*
1830.
By J. Pollard.

FIG. 32A.
Loading a Chaise and Pair,
c. 1800.
By W. H. Pyne.

FIG. 32B.
A Long Stage-Coach, *c.* 1800.
By W. H. Pyne.

CHAPTER II

THE EIGHTEENTH-CENTURY BUILDER

WE can now pass on to the building trade, which is the second of the three great trades we are considering, and it was a very important one indeed in the eighteenth century—kings, princes and nobles, as well as ordinary common or garden people, considered that it was necessary for them to know the rules of architecture as laid down by Andrea Palladio. He was an Italian architect, born in Vicenza in 1518, where he did most of his work, and died in 1580. His book " Quattro Libri dell' Architettura," was first published in Italy in 1570, and in England in 1676, and became the Bible of the Later Renaissance. Inigo Jones, the architect of the first completely Renaissance building in England, the Banqueting Hall, Whitehall, London, 1622, had a copy of Palladio which he annotated, and this is now in the Library of Worcester College, Oxford. Jones was in Italy in 1600, and again in 1613-14. In Palladio the Tuscan, Doric, Ionic, Corinthian and Composite Orders of Architecture, in the Roman manner, could be studied in detail, with all the parts properly proportioned, on the basis of the module, which was half the diameter of the column : and not only the Orders but the plans of buildings themselves, showing how the Italian architects had translated Roman details into bricks and mortar. Palladio, then, ranks with Vitruvius, of whom we had so much to say in our Greek books, and whose book was written about the time of Augustus, at the beginning of the Christian era. Palladio would have known Vitruvius' book, because there were many editions of it in the sixteenth, seventeenth and eighteenth centuries, and it was translated into many languages. One point is that Palladio was concerned with the Roman version of classical architecture.

So we come to the beginning of the eighteenth century, and we showed in Vol. II. of E.D.T. how far the English architects had advanced by the time Queen Anne was on the throne. We gave as an example of domestic architecture Fig. 96, of a house in the Close at Salisbury, and there is no better house of the middling type in England. We show the type again as A and B, Fig. 33, in this book. The pleasantly designed door and window over, as the central feature, with the sash windows with good fat bars, and sometimes slightly bevelled glass as at Hampton Court, on either side all under the roof, with its good cornice, as a brim to the hat, and the wrought-iron railings across the front, go to make up a pleasant picture in peaceful surroundings of English architecture at its very best. It was the genius of Wren, and the lesser men of the time, that made this possible. Wren was like some old alchemist—he could draw his details from Classical Rome, assimilate the notions of Dutch William and the practical requirements of an Englishman, and produce houses which were real homes, and this is more than can be said of some of the later palaces. Think of Belton House (1689), or the house at Chichester which is now the Council Offices, or Hampton Court itself, with its mellowed brick and stone —all are charming. At Hampton Court you have the ironwork of Jean Tijou (1690–1710), which led to a renaissance of that craft, shown in Fig. 71, Vol II.

You will find a full and lively account of this eighteenth-century building style, with the interiors and craftsmanship, in Sacheverell Sitwell's "British Architects and Craftsmen, 1600-1830." In the same "English Art and Building Series" full treatment is accorded in separate volumes to "The Age of Adam" by James Lees Milne, and to "The Regency Period" by Donald Pilcher.

The Fire of London helped forward this movement—of wood before, it was rebuilt after in brick, and the building trade benefited by the opportunity and set a fashion. Celia Fiennes, to whose journeys we refer in Vol. II., talks

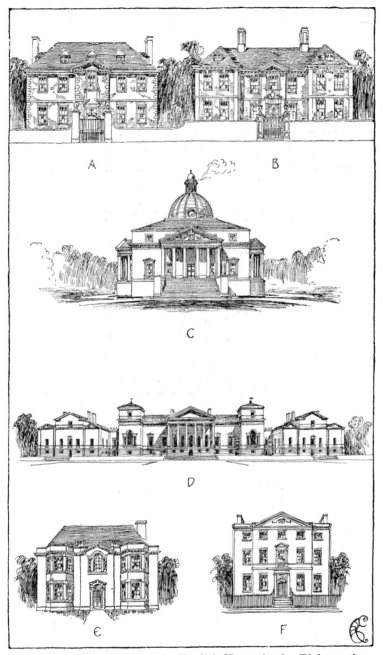

FIG. 33.—Evolution of the English House in the Eighteenth Century.

A.—The Moot, Downton, Wilts.
B.—Council Offices, Chichester, Sussex.
C.—Mereworth, Kent.
D.—Holkham Hall, Norfolk.
E.—At Lavenham, Suffolk, c. 1750.
F.—At St. Albans, c. 1785.

E*

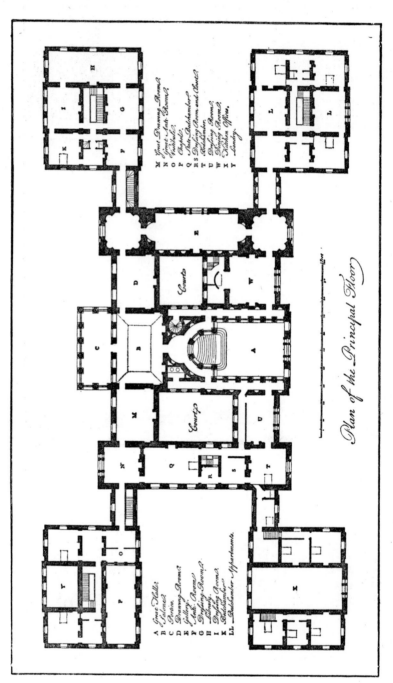

A Great Halls.
B Cabinet.
C Saloon.
D Drawing-Rooms.
E Gallery.
F State-Room.
G Dressing-Rooms.
H Library.
I Dressing-Rooms.
K Bedchamber.
LL Bedchamber Appartments.

M Great Drawing-Room.
N Great Ante-Room.
O Vestibule.
P Chapel.
Q State Bedchamber.
RS Dressing-Room and Closet.
T Bedchamber.
U Dressing-Rooms.
W Dressing-Room.
M Kitchen Offices.
Y Laundry.

Courts.

Courts.

Plan of the Principal Floor

Fig. 34.—Holkham Hall, Norfolk.   Plan of the Principal Floor.

of the houses built in the provinces in the "London manner."

Internally the houses of this period were as good as the exteriors. Rooms were panelled in oak, as Fig. 58 in Vol. II., which is one of the rooms at Belton—one run of panels under the dado rail, and one range of large panels over, and the doors and fireplaces very much part of the panelling, but enriched perhaps with carving from Grinling Gibbons's bench. The woodwork was superb, and can be seen by Londoners at St. Paul's, or in the City churches. The staircases were massive performances in wood. In the mid seventeenth century the balustrades were sometimes formed of flowing scrolls of acanthus, and we illustrated one of these in Vol. II., Fig. 59. The supporting string under was straight, and the steps were housed into this, which was called a Close String. Sometimes the balustrade was formed of large turned balusters. You can see many specimens in Gray's Inn and the Temple.

With the advent of the Georges a certain pomposity crept into planning, and people began to build in a grand rather than a comfortable manner. It is amazing now that any one man and his family can have contemplated living in the piles of masonry which date from this period.

Lord Burlington was the great patron of the Palladian movement. Burlington lived at Burlington House, in Piccadilly, and when our readers go to the Royal Academy they pass in under the new façade by Banks and Barry which replaces that designed by Colen Campbell, who lived with Burlington. The arcaded entrance and the Diploma Gallery on the top were also added much later. Colin Campbell published "Vitruvius Britannicus" (1715), and included the Burlington House front in it ; but far more important than this was Mereworth Castle, in Kent, as C, Fig. 33, which was illustrated as well in the third volume, published 1725. Campbell says this house was covered in in 1723.

The importance of the house is that it was an attempt to transplant pure Palladian architecture. Palladio in

his second book or chapter illustrated a villa that he had
built for a Monsignor Paolo Almerico, and Mereworth was
copied directly from this and surrounded by a moat.
Campbell says, "I shall not pretend to say that I have
made any improvements in this Plan from that of Palladio."
So Palladio was the architect's Bible, Holy Writ that must
not be altered. In the Palladian villa the four porticoes
and the central hall made cool places where the glare of
the southern sun could be avoided, but at Mereworth,
where only two are real porticoes, the only purpose they
served was to cut off the pale northern sun. Then fireplaces had to be added at Mereworth, and Palladian villas
are not improved by chimneys, so the twenty-four flues
were brought up in brick arches to discharge their smoke
out of the top of the dome (see Fig. 33).

Mereworth, then, is amazingly interesting, but it is the
beginning of the end. Neither Jones or Wren would have
designed in such a fashion. They were like those admirable
birds who, content to swallow almost anything, yet pre-
digest it before they beak it on to their young. So imagine
Lord Burlington and Campbell sitting together in Burlington House with Palladio open before them, and deter-
mining to try this Almerico villa on the Hon. John Fane,
who was the builder of Mereworth. He was amenable,
because Campbell says, "Never architect had a more
beneficent and liberal Patron"; and they were not
wantonly wicked, because Burlington built himself another
villa, at Chiswick, in 1727, in much the same manner.
Still they seemed to have tried it on the dog first.
Burlington was in Italy in 1718, and brought back with
him Kent, who was a young painter then, and was to
become an architect after his association with Burlington.
He lived in Burlington House—this was one of the nice
things of being a young architect in the eighteenth century ;
your clients not only provided you with jobs, but threw
in board and lodging.

Kent is thought to have helped with the interior

FIG. 35.—Staircase, with Chinese fret, John Street, Bedford Row,
London (1760).

decorations of Burlington House, and he published a book in 1727. A little later he was assisting Burlington, who was advising his friend, Thomas Coke, on the house he intended building at Holkham, in Norfolk. This was started in 1734, and the elevation is shown in D, Fig. 33, and the plan in Fig. 34, with an interior in Fig. 36A. This type of plan of a central block with outlying wings connected by corridors is better treated at Holkham than other examples, such as Kedleston, Derbyshire (1761), by Adam where the connecting corridors are much longer and curved in plan. Thomas Coke, who became the Earl of Leicester, died leaving no children, so that the estate passed to his grand-nephew, the great Coke of Norfolk, of whom we have written on p. 22.

James Gibbs, the architect of St. Martin's Church, Charing Cross, and St. Mary le Strand, another very gifted man, published a Book of Architecture in 1728—that was one of the troubles ; there were too many books, and the architects designed according to Palladian rules instead of practical considerations of comfort. Inside the houses in Palladian times the warm background of oak panelling gave way to plastered walls, with moldings planted on, and the doors and fireplaces, instead of being one with the walls, often stood apart by themselves as architectural compositions, complete with columns and entablatures, in the various orders. The ornament was far more architectural and mechanical than in Gibbons's day, with an inclination to rococo work sometimes.

In the eighteenth century the staircases began to have "cut strings"—that is, that the support was cut out to the shape of the stairs, and the balusters stood in groups of threes on each step. These were lighter than in the seventeenth century, and often beautifully turned in twists and spirals.

The Dilettanti (which did not mean then what it has come to mean now) Society was established in 1734 by five gentlemen who had travelled in Italy and wished to con-

FIG. 36.—In the Chinese manner, 1760.

(Bed and Dress from the Victoria and Albert Museum, London.)

tinue their studies. Italy was the source of inspiration. The Society of Arts was founded in 1753.

It was in 1741 that Horace Walpole returned from his Grand Tour, and he, for all his affection towards architecture, was to be one of the first to introduce doubt into the minds of the architects. The Palladian architects had carried on the Classical tradition, even if in a pompous way. Walpole was to suggest that they might follow a fashion instead and become Gothicists, or anything else which took their fancy. Walpole, in fact, was a Goth. It was in 1750 he wrote, " I am going to build a little Gothic Castle at Strawberry Hill," a house at Twickenham, Middlesex, which he had bought two years before. This is a long time before the Wyatts and Pugins were to attempt the impossible, but Walpole was not the first Goth. Lord Dacre had altered and enlarged Belhus, Essex, a Henry VIII. house, in the same style, in 1745, and Batty Langley brought out his " Gothic Architecture Restored and Improved " in 1742. Fig. 37 shows the staircase at Strawberry Hill with its " Gothic fretwork paper." Peter Atkinson, a York architect, added a " Gothick " front and gatehouse to Bishopthorpe, in York, the seat of the Archbishop of York, in 1765. Atkinson took an ordinary Georgian oblong building with a central pediment, and trimmed it up with a Gothic porch, battlements and arched windows. We find similar work at Arbury, Warwickshire, due to Sir Roger Newdigate, and at Milton House, near Didcot, 1764. There are also " Gothick " churches at Shobdon, Herefordshire, 1753, and at Croome d'Abitot, Worcestershire, c. 1760.

We have said these people were attempting the impossible, and their followers ever since have been doing the same thing. The real mediæval Gothic church and cathedral was the sign manual of a society constituted in such a way that it is far more foreign to us than those of Greece and Rome. We find it difficult to understand the Middle Ages, and mock Gothic architecture is consequently an artificial affair, though this " Rococo " Gothic can be

graceful and amusing. The work at Belhus is poor, thin
and lifeless. In one of the rooms Dacre put a classical
marble mantelpiece, which Walpole, who had gone there in
1754, noted as " one little miscarriage into total Ionic."
Another interesting thing at Belhus is that a new staircase,
built in 1745, was carried out in a better imitation of
Jacobean than the Gothic work. In one of the drawing-
rooms the walls were covered with canvas painted to look
like oak, and then on top Gothic arches and columns,
printed on paper, were cut out and pasted on to the background. " Capability " Brown was called in, and recom-
mended a 10-acre lake of " Form very irregular."

Still this early " Gothick " revival fitted in very well,
as all architecture does and must, with the spirit of the
time. People were beginning to be tired of classical rules
and wanted freedom and romance.

The opening to the fourth chapter of Henry Fielding's
" History of Tom Jones " (1749) is very interesting. We
are told that " The Gothic stile of building could produce
nothing nobler than Mr. Allworthy's house—it rivalled
the beauties of the best Grecian architecture." The
description of its surroundings strike the new romantic
note : there is a grove of old oaks—the lawns slope down—
springs gush out of fir-covered rocks, and cascades tumble
over mossy stones with lesser falls into a lake from which
a river winds its way to the sea. One of the prospects is
terminated by the ivy-clad towers of a ruined abbey, and
then the country (in Somerset) rises to a ridge of wild
mountains, the tops of which are above the clouds.

It was not the end, but it was the beginning of the
end, because from now on there were constantly changing
fashions in architecture, instead of continuous growth and
the feeling of permanence. Buildings, like a woman's hat,
looked foolish and old-fashioned in a year or so.

The Chinese fashion came into being because of the
ideas which Sir William Chambers brought back with him
from China. He published a book on Designs of Chinese

Buildings in 1753, and another on the Chinese work he did at Kew Gardens in 1763. The architects and furniture-makers managed this Chinese work a good deal better than the Gothic, and some of their interiors were very quaint and amusing, especially if the walls were covered with the hand-painted Chinese wall-papers which were imported about this time. Wall-papers started with patterns raised up in " flock," in imitation of hangings, but these were not much used until the middle of the eighteenth century. Figs. 35 and 36 show Chinese treatments. The staircase from John Street, Bedford Row, of about 1760, is very beautifully made of mahogany. The bed from the Victoria and Albert Museum is in black lacquer and gold.

These changing fashions were caused by many people being subjected to the awful trial of making money too quickly. The South Sea Bubble was the beginning of modern speculation and gambling. Still the Goths and the Chinese did not have it all their own way. Robert Adam came back from his Italian tour in 1758 and carried on the classical tradition, and became the leading architect, until he died in 1792, leaving behind him a peculiar impress on design. His death was followed by the declaration of war between England and France in 1793, and this closed a period both architecturally and politically.

Adam does not appear to have gone to Greece, but did go to Spalato, or Split as it is called now, in Dalmatia, and there made a study of the Palace of Diocletian. The Roman work here, though it is of the greatest interest because of the peculiar freedom with which the classical details are used, is very coarse in feeling, and without any of the delicacy of Adam's work. It would seem as if Adam must have gone to Pompeii when he was in Italy, and have been influenced as well by the publication of Stuart and Revett's book on the Antiquities of Athens in 1762, four years after Adam had set up in practice, and " Antiquités Etrusques Grecques et Romaines," published by Sir William Hamilton in Naples in 1766. Adam's work

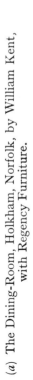

(a) The Dining-Room, Holkham, Norfolk, by William Kent, with Regency Furniture.

(b) Mecklenburgh Square, Bloomsbury.

FIGS. 36A, 36B—Contrasted Interiors: (a) Palladian, and (b) Regency.

FIG. 37.—Gothic Staircase at Strawberry Hill, Twickenham, *c.* 1750.
Designed by Horace Walpole.

By E. Edwards.

A. KEEPERS HOUSE WITH CHAPEL BEHIND ON 1ST FLOOR: B. TURNKEYS
LODGE: C. PRISONERS WARDS: D. OPEN YARDS: E. INFIRMARY
F. SEPARATE CELLS: G. PRESS YARD: H. CONDEMNED CELLS.
I. CONDEMNED ROOM: J. VISITORS ROOM: K. WOMENS YARD:
L. Do. FOR CONVICTED WOMEN WITH THEIR CONDEMNED ROOM AT M: VENT AREAS AT N.N.

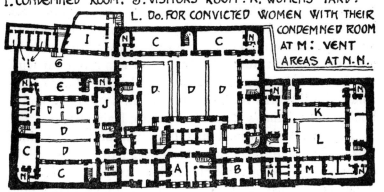

FIG. 38.—Newgate, from Britton and Pugin's " Public Buildings of London " (1838).

certainly had a Greek flavour. Wedgwood, who opened his works in 1769 and called them " Etruria," was another thus influenced, as was Flaxman, who worked with him.

Thomas Leverton (1743–1824) was another architect who followed the same tradition as Robert Adam; he designed the fine Woodhall Park, Hertfordshire (1778), and a lovely London town house at 1, Bedford Square (1775), with others there. Their smaller houses became much plainer outside—yellow bricks were used, and the cornices and string courses were all flatter. The sash bars of the windows were made much narrower as the century proceeded. Inside the typical Adam decorations were carried out in a composition of whitening and glue stuck on to the walls, and the flatness of this called for colouring, which was carried out in very light tints of delicate greens and blues, lilacs and dove greys, and faint yellows. Set in these painted walls were very beautiful mahogany doors, and this wood began to be used about 1720. The typical Adam fireplace was made of marble and inlaid in a very dainty fashion. Stone staircases began to be used in houses with very beautiful wrought-iron balusters set into them

F   51

supporting a light mahogany handrail; later on cast-iron balustrades were used by Robert Adam.

But Adam must not be thought of as a mere decorator; he was a brilliant planner of state rooms and could fit great bows and apses, and work in the twists of his compass with anybody. He was no mere copyist; all the information he gathered passed through his brain and was given out with the true Adam impress. He and his brother James published the "Works in Architecture" in 1778–1824, and a book on Diocletian's Palace in Spalato, Dalmatia, in 1764.

Bay windows, which had been out of fashion since Elizabethan and Jacobean times, began to be used again about the middle of the eighteenth century, as E, Fig. 33. F shows a house of 1785, and it should be noted how towards the end of the century the attics, which earlier had been placed in the roof, were now given outside walls of their own, so that the house becomes higher.

Sir William Chambers, whose book on Civil Architecture was published in 1759, carried on the more masculine traditions of the Palladian school, and his best-known work is Somerset House, in London (1776).

Henry Holland (b. 1746, d. 1806) was another architect who designed with delicate elegance, with a slight French touch. Brooks Club in London is by him; like others Carlton House vanished (in 1824) but is seen in Pyne's "Royal Residences". He worked at Althorp, Northamptonshire, and designed Broadlands, Romsey, and Southill, Bedfordshire, for the Whitbreads.

Now we come to the work of a man who produced one terrific masterpiece, and as it was a prison, and as most of us, with luck, keep out of prison, we have added notes on its use, so that the architectural solution of the problem and the mental attitude of the time may be understood.

The masterpiece was Newgate Prison, London, which was pulled down in 1903 to make way for the present Central Criminal Court. Newgate was the work of George Dance, one of the sons of the City Surveyor who designed

FIG. 39.—The Debtor's Door, Newgate Prison, London, in 1821.

(George Dance, Architect, 1770.)

FIG. 40.—The Condemned Sermon, Newgate Chapel, 1809.

By Pugin and Rowlandson.

the Mansion House. Born in 1741, he went to study architecture in Italy in 1758 and, returning to England in 1764, set up in practice. In 1768 he was elected as one of the original members of the R.A., and he was commissioned to design Newgate. The buildings, started in 1770, were nearly destroyed by fire in the Gordon Riots in 1780, and finally remodelled, improved, and completed in 1782. The extraordinary thing about George Dance is that while his other work, like All Hallows Church, London Wall, and St. Luke's Hospital, Old Street, were scholarly buildings, Newgate had the indubitable hall-mark of genius about it. Think of the difficulties of the problem—the site had a frontage of about 130 feet to Newgate Street, and 300 feet to the Old Bailey. Dance put the keeper's house in the centre of the long side (see Fig. 38); behind came the chapel, on the first floor. The north or Newgate Street end of the building was occupied at first by debtors, male and female. There was an internal courtyard, divided up by low walls, which are shown on the plan, and around these yards came the wards in which the debtors lived, rising three storeys above the pavement. In Ackermann's "Microcosm of London" (1808) it states that a room of 23 feet by 15 was usually occupied by fifteen to twenty people. The plan at the south end was much the same, and was occupied by felons and persons confined for offences against the Government.

If our readers, after having studied the plan (Fig. 38), will turn to our chapter on Sanitation and realize what the sanitary conditions of buildings were like in London in the early nineteenth century, they will understand why gaol fever was rampant in Newgate, with its narrow courts and lack of drainage. Conditions inside the gaols were terrible, and the fettered prisoners not only died themselves, but were a source of danger to the citizens when brought into court. Fig. 41 shows the Justice Hall, commonly called the Sessions House, which adjoined Newgate, where the prisoners were brought to trial through a passage. Ackermann

FIG. 41.—The Sessions House, Old Bailey, London, in 1809.

illustrates the Court, and says that it had been " rebuilt entirely of stone . . . and that every precaution has been taken to render it airy, and to prevent the effect of the effluvia arising from that dreadful disorder, the gaol fever." The prisons were farmed out to people for profit, and the keeper charged exorbitant fees. Poor Cobbett had to pay £12 12s. a week (see p. 113). John Howard, the great prison reformer, had visited gaols at the end of the eighteenth century and drawn attention to their terrible condition. He pointed out that the real use of a prison was to reform the criminals and train them to habits of industry, but the war prevented reform and it was not till after 1815 that any progress was made, due mainly to the Quakers. Gaol Acts were passed in 1823–24, and Inspectors of Prisons appointed condemned Newgate as a monstrous place, and about 1835 Pentonville Prison, with its tiers of separate cells, radiating like the spokes of a wheel, became the accepted type.

To revert to Newgate, one thing to note in Fig. 38 (which, by the way, dates from Britton and Pugin, " Public Buildings," 1838) is how the prison, with the exception of the Keeper's House, looked inwards on itself, not outwards on the world. Through no window could the unfortunate felon see his more fortunate fellows who were free, and what is curious, Dance seems to have been helped by this, because the windowed Keeper's House was the least satisfactory part of the design. In our drawing (Fig. 39) just the edge of the Keeper's House shows on the left. In the centre is the Debtors' Door, and on the right the end of the Felons' Blocks. Here and at the debtors' end, and on the return frontage to Newgate Street, the walls rose sheer up to the cornice in plain rusticated blocks of masonry, and the only relief was the niches we have shown, deeply shadowed and housing rather gay eighteenth-century figures. These figures always seemed to us a grim jest because of their gaiety. One held a cap of Liberty, and another a cornucopia with fruit and flowers, and the

FIG. 42.—Knocking off the Irons in the Press Yard, Newgate, 1821. (After Cruikshank.)

inhabitants were not free, and the harvest garnered in Newgate was a sad and sorry one—as one looked at the figures the building became grimmer. Relief was given to the composition by breaking back the line of the walling around the Debtors' Door as shown in Fig. 39, and another of similar design on the north side of the Keeper's House, and these doorways Dance treated in a very satisfactory way, from the architectural point of view; and here he used leg-irons and fetters and chains as an ornament. And there was nothing more than this—no shams anywhere —just the great sombre walls shadowed by their heavy cornices, and practically the entire face of the building had been pitted with the mason's chisels into what is called a "rusticated" surface, and the London soot had found lodgment in the rustications, which added to the sombreness except where, here and there, the surface of the Portland stone had been bleached white by sun and rain.

It was impossible to pass Newgate without a lowering of the spirit—it spoke of man's inhumanity to man. How Dance managed it we cannot say—perhaps as a young man

FIG. 43.—The East Front of Ayot St. Lawrence Church, Hertfordshire.

(*Nicholas Revett, Architect,* 1788.)

FIG. 44.—Interior of Ayot St. Lawrence Church, Hertfordshire.
(*Nicholas Revett, Architect,* 1788.)

coming back fresh from Italy he remembered the heavy walls of the Palazzo Strozzi, or the Pitti in Florence, and, taking them from the sun, achieved the results in our grey gloom ; or he may have been influenced by the extraordinary prison drawings published by Piranesi in 1751. In this "Carceri" series the great Italian draughtsman "let himself go," and in interminable staircases and endless corridors showed poor humans struggling for freedom denied to them. Dance himself was a very fine draughtsman.

Fig. 40 shows the chapel at Newgate during service on the Sunday preceding the execution of criminals. Quoting from Ackermann's "Microcosm," we are told that : "Upon this occasion, a suitable sermon, called *the condemned sermon*, is preached by the ordinary ; during which a coffin is placed on a table within an inclosure, called the Dock ; and round this coffin are prisoners condemned to die." The public were admitted at charges varying from 6*d.* to 2*s.*, the money received being the perquisite of the turnkeys.

Fig. 42 shows the Press Yard in Newgate on the morning of an execution. The yard was long and narrow, and contained a great number of cells one above another, three stories in all. Each cell measured 9 feet by 6 feet. When the death warrant arrived at Newgate the prisoners to die were allowed the freedom of the yard, and here the clergyman attended them, and generally sat up praying with them all the night before the execution. In the letterpress describing the plate in *London Life*, from which we have drawn Fig. 42, the figure on the left talking to the parson is said to be "Lively Jem," who ran through a fine fortune before coming to a sad end. His leg-irons have been removed in the same way as those of his sturdy companion. The Yeoman of the Halter is in waiting to put the ropes about them, and the Sheriffs are in attendance to see that the sentence is carried out ; meanwhile the tolling bell added "a terrific solemnity to the proceedings."

Then the procession was formed and passed out of the

Debtors' Door to find the scaffold erected in the Old Bailey, as shown in Fig. 39. Again quoting from Ackermann, we read that " The mode of executing criminals at Tyburn had long been complained of, as tending rather to introduce depravity, by a want of solemnity, than to operate as a preventive to crimes, by exhibiting an awful example of punishment. To remedy this evil, both the place and manner of execution were changed : a temporary scaffold was constructed, to be placed in the open space before the debtors' door of Newgate, having a movable platform for the criminals to stand on, which, by means of a lever and rollers, falls from under them. The whole of this building is hung with black ; and the regulations which are observed on these mournful occasions, are calculated to produce that impression on the minds of the spectators which is the true end of all punishments."

We know now that public executions attracted the worst elements in the population. It was one of the things to do. The night of waiting was spent in drinking to pass the time, until the dawn came and the poor wretches passed out of the Debtors' Door to their doom. By 1840 people were only hanged for murder, but they were hanged publicly till 1868.

Now look once more on Dance's design for Newgate and see how well he realized all this in stone. Perhaps it is just as well that Newgate was pulled down. The building which succeeded it, if very poor architecture, is at all events rather kindlier in appearance.

We are interested in Newgate, and have illustrated it rather fully, because it enables us to understand a side of late eighteenth and early nineteenth-century character which seems very remote to us, and that is their treatment of criminals. If we take the words of Mr. Lewis E. Lawes, our ideal should be to make the criminal " unskilled worker to learn a trade ; the illiterate to acquire the education needed to hold a job ; the wanderer to find for himself a home and responsibility ; the deficient mentally

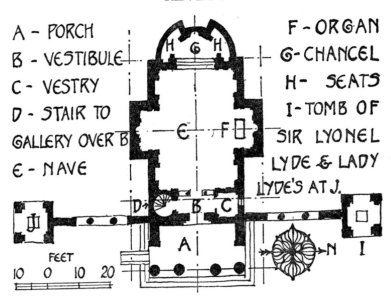

A – PORCH

B – VESTIBULE

C – VESTRY

D – STAIR TO
GALLERY OVER B

E – NAVE

F – ORGAN

G – CHANCEL

H – SEATS

I – TOMB OF
SIR LYONEL
LYDE & LADY
LYDE'S AT J.

FEET
10 0 10 20

FIG. 45.—Plan of Ayot St. Lawrence Church, Hertfordshire.

to attain a better understanding of the values of life ; the
cynic and perverse to adopt a saner attitude towards society
and government "—reformation rather than punishment.

In the early nineteenth century it was punishment, and
capital punishment, not only for murder, but theft and
forgery, and as it was the law of the land it met with
general acceptance. It is quite wrong to judge our fore-
fathers by twentieth-century standards. We still retain
capital punishment for murder, and Mr. Lawes in his book
" 20,000 Years in Sing Sing " says that he has " been
directed to kill lawfully one hundred and fifty men and one
woman," and his experience has convinced him of the
futility of capital punishment. So in a few years books
may be written on lawful killing as a thing of the past.

Now we shall have to go back to p. 51, where we
suggested that Robert Adam was influenced in the detail
of his work by the publication of Stuart and Revett's book
on the Antiquities of Athens in 1762. Beyond this the

book does not appear to have had very much influence at the time of its publication. The Palladian tradition was too strong, and Walpole's " Gothick " caught the public favour first. At the end of the century though, and the beginning of the nineteenth, the Greek Revival was in full blast, and Stuart and Revett came into their own.

Nicholas Revett, born about 1721, was the son of a Suffolk squire. He went to Rome in 1742 and became acquainted there with James Stuart. He was the son of a Scottish sailor, and was born in 1713. While in Rome the two men decided to go on to Athens, and there they made the drawings for their book. Any design, then, by either Stuart or Revett must be of interest, because we can see if they practised what they preached. The building we have selected is a church designed by Revett in 1788.

To find it we shall have to try and persuade such of our readers as can to go to Ayot St. Lawrence, in Hertford-shire. This village is to be found in the pleasant winding lanes of the country to the west of Welwyn, of Garden City fame. You could on the same day see both Ayot and Welwyn, and so be able to contrast the old and new. But the particular attraction at Ayot St. Lawrence, so far as we are concerned, is that you can contrast two kinds of churches there. First there is the original church of St. Lawrence, which gave its name to the village. The nave is twelfth century, the north aisle is thirteenth ; the chancel and north chapel are fourteenth, and the tower fifteenth century, but the church is now ruinous, and ivy is tearing the walls to pieces. Yet as a ruin the old church is part and parcel of the countryside, and as much at home as the cottages of the villagers.

We shall find the church, built by Sir Lyonel Lyde in 1788, in the park of Ayot House. It can be seen from the road, and there is a public footpath across the park to the churchyard; we approach the east or entrance front shown in Fig. 43. This is strange, because the Christian practice is to have the entrance at the west. The roof of the nave is covered with copper which has turned a lovely verdigris green, and the walls are stuccoed with plaster. As we come nearer the strange classical façade reveals itself as one of great interest, but there is nothing to denote that it is a church—it might be a mausoleum or a dozen other things, and the only Christian symbols are the crosses over the graves in the churchyard. If the sun is shining and the sky is blue the total effect is happy, but if the day is grey and the rain falling the building looks dismal and sad, and like some poor Pan who has gone piping through the woods and lost his way and strayed into a foreign country, so foreign that his friend Echo and attendant nymphs have deserted him. That is the fault with this very interesting building of Revett's—it is an importation from the sunny land of Greece, and not really at home. If we go into the church the first thing which strikes us is the disproportionate size of the porch. If we look at the plan, Fig. 45, we see that the porch is nearly half the size of the nave. We saw the beginnings of this porch in the Megaron at Tiryns, and the house at Priene, and the pronaos or portico of the Parthenon, (Everyday Things in Ancient Greece), but in the sunny climate of Greece the portico was used as a very agreeable outdoor sitting-room, and it was added to their temples because these were the homes of their gods; if the people needed porticoes where they could take the air, so did the gods. So the portico which was reasonable in Greece is foolish at Ayot St. Lawrence.

The actual interior of the church (as Fig. 44) is again of the greatest interest, but it would do just as well for a banking hall; the organ is rather a beauty and appears to be original, but someone has Gothicized the communion table surroundings and added stained glass windows which are not happy; nor is the modern font in the Wren manner, and manner only. To sum up, then, the fault with the Church is, that it represents drawing-board architecture; it was designed, and did not grow out of the soil. It is foreign and not indigenous. But this is a late and extreme example of Greek classic;

we must not get the Gothic revival idea that all churches in this century were Pagan ; there were many examples of varied design quite appropriate for congregational worship, from great town building to humble village fanes, such as Horbury, Yorkshire, Binley, Warwickshire, Badminton, Gloucestershire, and Hardenhuish, Wiltshire, as we see in Marcus Whiffen's " Stuart and Georgian Churches " (1603–1837) issued in 1948, in which he shows for the first time the course of design in Renaissance country buildings.

Sir Lyonel Lyde was buried in the right-hand pavilion of the entrance front, and Lady Lyde in the left-hand. The English inscription on the front of his memorial says that he died on June 22nd, 1791, in the sixty-eighth year of his age, and on the back is a Latin inscription, which explains the building : " Nicholas Revett of Suffolk who spent many years in Rome, Athens and Smyrna, designed, built, and decorated this church according to the examples of ancient architecture which are yet to be seen in Greece and Asia Minor and raised this monument at the expense of Sir Lyonel Lyde Baronet A.D. 1788."

Neither Stuart nor Revett appears to have done very much architectural work. The house in St. James's Square, London, now occupied by the Clerical Life Assurance, is one of Stuart's best works. It has very fine rich interiors.

Robert Adam also remodelled a Georgian church at Mistley in Essex. With its two towers and cupolas it was like an extra-magnificent stable block. Unfortunately it gave way in 1870 to a " neat edifice in the Early Decorated style," but the two towers remain as navigational landmarks. The general effect can be judged from the engravings in Adam's " Works." (p. 76).

That is perhaps all we need say of eighteenth-century building. There was the Palladian tradition still carried on by Chambers and Dance, the more delicate work of Adam and his school, the " Gothick " of Walpole, the " Chinese " of Chambers, and the " Greek " of Stuart and Revett.

CHAPTER III

CLOTHING

THE third great trade is that of the clothier, and in the Northern Hemisphere, with its rigorous climate, it is a very important one indeed. In the Old Stone Age man was a hunter, and clothed himself and his family with the skins of the animals he killed, and sewed them together with sinews, punching holes with a bone awl and pulling the sinew through with another like a crotchet hook. We illustrated his outfit in Everyday Life Series, Vol. I—but man did not weave in the Old Stone Age.

In the New Stone Age he learned to domesticate some of the animals, and by the Bronze Age was spinning and weaving their fleeces into cloth. If our readers care to consult Mr. Ling Roth's books they will find how widespread an art weaving has been. The loom on which Penelope wove the shroud for Laertes is illustrated on Greek vases, and, excepting that it is vertical instead of horizontal, the principles on which it worked are the same as the eighteenth century A.D. one illustrated in Fig. 47. Nobody in all the centuries had been hurried or worried; they wove as their fathers had and were content with trifling alterations and improvements—but the loom was not to escape. We have seen that in 1733 Jethro Tull brought out his book and revolutionized the practice of Agriculture; in the same year John Kay of Bury

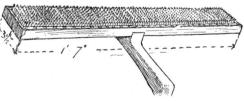

FIG. 46.—Carding Implement.

63

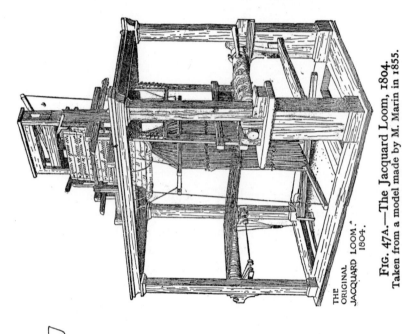

THE
ORIGINAL
JACQUARD LOOM.
1804.

FIG. 47A.—The Jacquard Loom, 1804.
Taken from a model made by M. Marin in 1855.
(*Manchester School of Technology.*)

WARP
THREADS

HEALDS

HEALD
SHAFTS

BATTEN

REED

SHED

WARP
BEAM

CLOTH
BEAM

TREADLES

FIG. 47.—The Hand Loom up till A.D. 1733.
(*Science Museum, London.*)

Fig. 48.—Original Spinning Machine
(Arkwright), 1769.

(*Science Museum, London.*)

Fig. 49.—Spitalfield's Hand Loom with Jacquard.

(*Science Museum, London.*)

FIG. 50.—Replica of Crompton's " Mule " (1774–9).
(*Science Museum, London.*)

FIG. 51.—Replica of Hargreave's Spinning Jenny (1750–57).
(*Science Museum, London.*)

FIG. 52.—The Hand-Weaver's Shuttle, 9⅞ inches long.
(*Science Museum, London.*)

invented the flying-shuttle, and as this immensely increased the speed of weaving the whole trade was dis-
organized, with tremendous dislocations and alterations in
the lives of the people. To understand this it may be as
well to take stock of the position before Kay's invention.

We cannot deal with all the processes in cleaning and

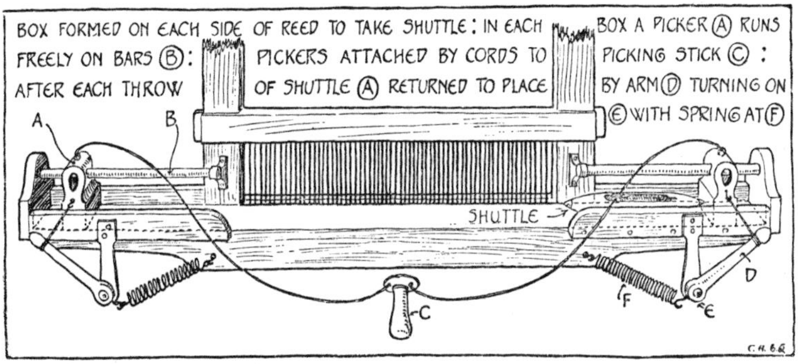

FIG. 53.—John Kay's Flying Shuttle, 1733.
(*Science Museum, London.*)

preparing the wool or cotton before it is spun, but the final
one was by the use of carding instruments, as Fig. 46, to
arrange the fibres of the material lengthways, loosely
rolled into a very delicate rope-like form called a roving.
Until Hargreaves invented his spinning jenny (1750–7)
this was spun into thread on a spinning wheel, as Fig. 140.

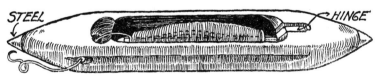

FIG. 54.—The Weaver's Shuttle, 12 inches long, Early 19th Century.
(*Science Museum, London.*)

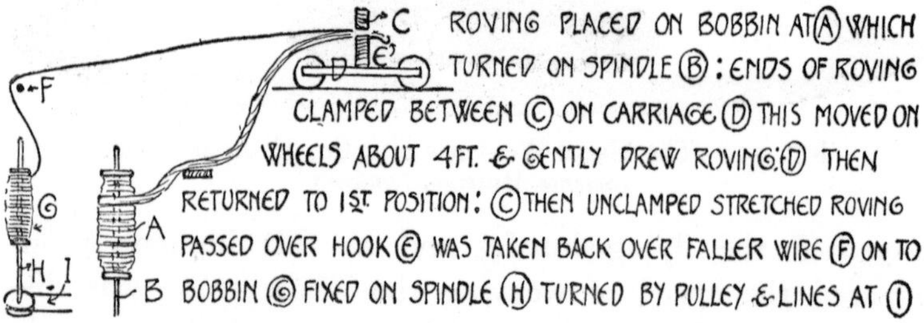

C ROVING PLACED ON BOBBIN AT Ⓐ WHICH
TURNED ON SPINDLE Ⓑ : ENDS OF ROVING
CLAMPED BETWEEN Ⓒ ON CARRIAGE Ⓓ THIS MOVED ON
WHEELS ABOUT 4 FT. & GENTLY DREW ROVING: Ⓓ THEN
RETURNED TO 1ST POSITION : Ⓒ THEN UNCLAMPED STRETCHED ROVING
PASSED OVER HOOK Ⓔ WAS TAKEN BACK OVER FALLER WIRE Ⓕ ON TO
BOBBIN Ⓖ FIXED ON SPINDLE Ⓗ TURNED BY PULLEY & LINES AT Ⓘ

FIG. 55.—The Mechanical Part of Hargreave's Spinning Jenny.

This interesting little machine—for machine it was—had been introduced into England in the sixteenth century. The rovings were placed on a distaff and paid out by hand on to a bobbin on a horizontal spindle turned by foot pedal. One very important detail to be remembered is that the material to be spun was not put on to the distaff in one mass, like cotton-wool, but had already, by means of the cards, been turned into the continuous roving, and the function of the hand was to draw out this roving and give it the necessary stretch which settled the thickness of the thread, and the spinning wheel spun *one thread at a time.*

We can now pass on to the loom before 1733, as Fig. 47. The long threads called the warp were put on the warp beam or roller at the back, and then brought forward as shown to the healds—here each warp thread was passed through a loop on the healds ; the healds were attached to heald shafts, and here was a very simple but ingenious bit of mechanism. From the two treadles under came two cords, one attached under each heald shaft. From the tops of the heald shafts went four cords attached to two little yokes suspended on two cords, and free to move up and down like seesaws on them. In Fig. 47, of the four cords shown between the yokes and the heald shafts, the two outer cords are attached to the front heald shaft, and the two inner cords to the back heald shaft.

It is easy to see that with this arrangement if one treadle were depressed one heald would go up, and one down, and as the warp threads went through eyes on the healds one set of threads went up, and one down. When the other treadle was used another set of threads could be raised and lowered to form the shed or space through which the shuttle was passed. The warp threads were passed through the vertical wires of the reed, and this was arranged on a swinging batten, and banged the weft threads from the shuttle tightly together to form the cloth. This when woven passed on to the cloth beam, which had handles on it so that the material could be rolled up.

The actual process of weaving consisted of throwing the shuttle through the shed with the right hand, say, and catching it with the left. The batten was then swung forward and returned back before the shuttle was thrown through the shed again, this time with the left hand. Fig. 52 shows the type of shuttle used, with its pirn or bobbin.

This was how spinning and weaving was done before 1733, and as the development had been gradual there was a nice balance about the business; and balance is an essential quality. We can explain what we mean by taking the see-saw as an example; an 8-stone boy 5 feet from the centre will balance a 5-stone boy 8 feet from the centre. If either moves a foot in, bang down goes the other. Life since 1733 has been unbalanced; first one

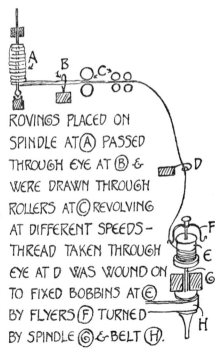

ROVINGS PLACED ON SPINDLE AT (A) PASSED THROUGH EYE AT (B) & WERE DRAWN THROUGH ROLLERS AT (C) REVOLVING AT DIFFERENT SPEEDS — THREAD TAKEN THROUGH EYE AT D WAS WOUND ON TO FIXED BOBBINS AT (E) BY FLYERS (F) TURNED BY SPINDLE (G) & BELT (H).

FIG. 56.—The Mechanical Part of Arkwright's Spinning Machine.

67

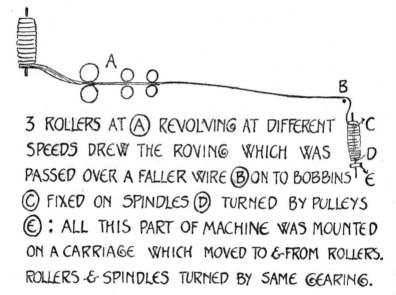

3 ROLLERS AT (A) REVOLVING AT DIFFERENT
SPEEDS DREW THE ROVING WHICH WAS
PASSED OVER A FALLER WIRE (B) ON TO BOBBINS
(C) FIXED ON SPINDLES (D) TURNED BY PULLEYS
(E) : ALL THIS PART OF MACHINE WAS MOUNTED
ON A CARRIAGE WHICH MOVED TO &-FROM ROLLERS.
ROLLERS &-SPINDLES TURNED BY SAME GEARING.

FIG. 57.—Mechanical part of Crompton's " Mule."

thing and then another has happened, which has either
banged you on the ground or left you shuddering up in the
air wondering what was going to happen next.

Now one of the prime causes of all this was Kay's
flying shuttle. Fig. 53 shows this, and it is the most
innocent-looking contraption. All the weaver had to do
was to hold the picking stick in his right hand and, with
a quick jerk, throw the shuttle through the shed. The
warp strings forming the bottom of the shed came through
the reed on the top of the beam under it. The left hand
was free to swing the batten, so it is easy to understand
that the speed of weaving was increased. Each throw of
the shuttle is called a pick; hence picking-stick. The
shuttles sometimes had four wheels under. Fig 54 shows
a later type.

Kay's flying shuttle was the beginning of industrial
discontent, because it upset the balance of things. The
next step came when James Hargreaves, a poor weaver of
Blackburn, saw his wife's spinning wheel upset on the floor,

where it continued to spin. In this position its horizontal spindle would have been upright, and Hargreaves evidently thought: Why not drive the spindles upright, and why not drive more than one? This he did in his spinning Jenny, so named because that was his wife's name, and Fig. 51 shows a replica of the original machine in the Science Museum. As this looks far more complicated than it is in reality we have prepared a diagram in Fig. 55 which explains the principle. The various parts are noted by the same letters in Fig. 51.

In the original spinning wheel which Har-

FIG. 58.—Riding Dress (1774).

greaves' wife used she thinned out the roving to the required thinness to make the thread by pulling it off the distaff by hand. In Hargreaves' Jenny he did this with his travelling carriage D, and he must have watched this part of the work carefully. Spinning it after this was much the same on the jenny as on the wheel, except that the spindle was vertical instead of horizontal. Hargreaves was experimenting with his jenny between 1750 and 1757, and patented it in 1770. He earned no gratitude by his invention, because the spinners by this time had caught up with the flying shuttles and so could keep pace with the weavers.

69

As the jenny could spin 120 threads at a time against the hand spinner's one, the spinners thought that large numbers of them would be rendered unemployed by the jenny, so they broke up Hargreaves' machines, and he had to fly for his life to Nottingham.

FIG. 59.—Housekeeper (1777). White muslin cap, large ruffled frill.

The next step was taken by Richard Arkwright, and he must be noted as another of the amateurs who did good work. Born in 1732, he became a barber, and going round the mills to fit his customers with wigs he heard talk of the many attempts which were being made at the time to improve spinning and weaving methods ; so he determined to try his hand at it, and produced his first spinning machine in 1769. This is now at the Science Museum London, and next to it there is the improved type made by Arkwright about 1775. We have shown the one of 1769 in Fig. 48, though it has lost some of its parts, because it has the great interest of being the original conception. Arkwright drove his machines, or frames, by water power ; hence they are sometimes called water frames. The principle is explained in Fig. 56. It will be remembered that Hargreaves drew out his roving by attaching it to a travelling carriage. Arkwright did his drawing by passing the roving through pairs of rollers revolving at different speeds— the under roller was grooved

FIG. 60.
Country Woman (1777). Muslin cap, wool cloak.

FIG 61.
Parasol. Cane stick 1¾ yds. long, green silk, brown fringe

70

steel, and the upper one wood covered with leather. The thread was then wound on to bobbins as shown in Fig. 56. Paul had experimented with rollers in 1738, but his machines had not been successful. Arkwright was a clever and business-like man, and built up a large fortune and became Sir Robert. One great advantage of his frame was that it spun a cotton thread sufficiently strong to be used for warp, which hitherto had had to be spun in flax. Fig. 48 shows that

FIG. 62.—Silk Sack Dress (1775–85). (*Victoria and Albert Museum, London.*)

in appearance it was more like a gate-legged table than a machine.

Samuel Crompton of Bolton followed with the machine which he designed between 1774–9, and as it was a combination of Hargreaves' jenny and Arkwright's rollers it was called a mule. Fig. 50 shows a replica of the mule in the Science Museum, London. Fig. 57 explains the principle. Crompton did not do much good for himself with his mule, and seems to have been jockeyed out of receiving any benefit.

All these spinning inventions had enabled the spinners

FIG. 63.—Dress of Striped Poplin with a Quilted Petticoat (1780–95).

FIG. 64.—Riding Dress with Velvet Skirt (1780–95).
(*Victoria and Albert Museum, London.*)

to catch up the weavers, so times were ripe for new developments. These came with the invention of the power-loom by the Rev. Edmund Cartwright, D.D., in 1785. The weaving principle remained the same, as can be seen by the power loom of 1851 which is illustrated in Fig. 138. It was the application of power, first by means of a bull, and then, in 1789, by a steam-engine, which was revolutionary and affected not only weaving but the planning of towns and the general life of the people. We discuss this in the next chapter.

As to the clothes which were made of the materials woven on the looms we have described, we gave the general development of dress in the eighteenth century in Vol. II, so that it seems to us in this Vol. III all we need do is to add some details.

FIG. 65A.—Skating in 1784.
(*After Rowlandson.*)

FIG. 66.—Dress about 1785.
(*Victoria and Albert Museum, London.*)

Readers of the Woodforde Diary may be glad to know that when Mrs. Howes appeared in her silk sack in 1778 she must have looked like Fig. 62, and Nancy might easily have worn the dress in Fig. 63. See also Fig. 65.

Fig. 67 shows an amusing form of headcovering called a calash, worn outdoors as a protection, and

. *opposite—*
f Spitalfields Silk with Pink Satin Quilted Petticoat, *c.* 1875.

FIG. 67.—Calash (late Eighteenth
Century).
(*Victoria and Albert Museum, London.*)

made of whale-bone and
silk. Woodforde gave his
sister and Nancy the black
and white silk hat-bands
worn at funerals to makes
calashes.

Fig. 69 shows a riding
habit, which must have
looked more like a livery
than a dress. The habit
was of blue cloth, with gold
buttons and a gold braid belt.
The stock was blue. The black
hat had cock's feathers and
a gold band, and underneath
it was worn a black curled wig,
and the lady wore yellow boots.
This can be truthfully described
as " some outfit." The lady on
the right is Grecian, and so that
there can be no mistake her
bonnet follows the lines of
Athene's helmet. Underneath a
flaxen wig was worn. The white
muslin dress was embroidered
with green and red, and pink
shoes and gloves built up a pretty
ensemble.

FIG. 68.—White Muslin
Dress with Cherry Ribbon.
(*Heideloff Gallery of Fashions*, 1764)

74

FIG. 69.—Riding and Walking Dress.
(*Heideloff Gallery of Fashions,* 1799.)

Fig. 71A—which our publisher has kindly allowed us to
have in colour—shows the interesting development which
took place in the design of special dresses for wearing on
the new-fashioned seaside holidays.   The first lady on the
left wears a white India calico overdress, with muslin under,
and on her head a mob cap under, and then a straw bonnet
over, with a green silk detachable eye-shade stiffened with
wire.   The same headdress is repeated on the second lady,
and her dress is all in muslin, with a blue silk underbodice.
The third lady has a Dunstable straw bonnet over a laced

75

cap, a striped gingham gown, and a white Norwich shawl, probably made of wool. All the shoes were of gaily-coloured morocco. The unfortunate female infants are replicas of mamma, and any boy of to-day dressed as the one in Fig. 71A would die of shame. As to the young women, doubtless the young men found them attractive. It is a little bit unfair; the young girl can wear almost anything and yet not lose her charm.

Here we should like to recommend our readers to pay a visit to the Dress Gallery at the Victoria and Albert Museum, South Kensington, London. Here is a wonderful procession of figures, all clothed in the real clothes of all the times, from James i down to the present day, and in cases at the sides are the little etceteras like lace, and shoes, and so on. The Gallery gives one a splendid idea of the development of dress. There are other good collections at the Bethnal Green and the London Museums.

FIG. 70.—Mistley Church, Essex. Designed by Robert Adam. The church was demolished in 1870; the towers remain.
(For notes v. p. 62.)

CHAPTER IV

THE SUBSIDIARY TRADES :
TRANSPORT, POWER AND HEALTH

TRANSPORT.—We saw in Vol. II what difficulties Celia Fiennes had to encounter when she went on her travels in England in the seventeenth century. How near Leicester she found " very deep bad roads. . . . I was near 11 hours going but 25 mile "—and that on horseback. Turnpikes had started at the close of the Stuart epoch, and progress was made in the eighteenth century ; still there were many gaps. Because of the bad roads, which made wheeled traffic impossible, pack-horses were used, and carried 280 lb. of coal, for one example, in panniers on their backs.

Then it occurred to the Duke of Bridgewater to make a canal between his coal pits at Worsley and Manchester. There had been river traffic before, but not canals, so two Acts of Parliament were obtained in 1759–60, and Bridgewater set his engineer, James Brindley, to work. Here is a thing to note : the tide of invention stimulated men's minds to an extraordinary extent. They had no data to go on—no standards—no gauges—yet they went out into the blue and performed the most wonderful feats of construction.

An engineer to-day, on the strength of what these men did, knows the strength of all his materials, and their sizes and qualities. The early engineers may have been devoid of any sense of beauty and fitness, as many are to-day, alas ! but they were plucky and inspired builders. Take the aqueduct over the Irwell, as Fig. 72, which enabled Brindley to dispense with many locks ; it would be quite a feat to-day, and must have seemed a miracle when it was constructed in 1761. The later viaduct over the River Medlock and the Ashton Canal, as Fig. 74, is an involved and difficult piece of construction.

Brindley had been a millwright, and though we should call him illiterate he was a great genius. His method of working, when confronted with a difficult problem, was to go to bed for a few days and think it out. When he knew what he was going to do he got up and did it.

As a result of Bridgewater's canals coal fell from 7d. per cwt. in Manchester to 3½d. This success led to many more canals, which were used for the transport of all kinds of goods. Pottery, which used to get damaged on the backs of the pack-horses, travelled quite safely by canal (see Fig. 72). Inland navigation was the term used, so the men who made the canals were called navvies.

So much for the transport of goods. When people travelled, they used the roads, because there was nothing else to use. When Woodforde went to Weston to take up his residence there he rode on horseback, first from Somerset to Oxford, and then on to Norfolk, by way of Thame and Tring, where he struck Icknield Way, the oldest road in England, and followed this to Dunstable, Baldock, Royston and so on. For years afterwards he rides, hiring a chaise for his niece when she wanted to go calling.

When they went to Somerset together for their holiday, May, 1782, they went by the London coach, which started from Norwich at nine o'clock at night and reached London at two on the next afternoon. Two inside places cost £1 16s., and one outside one for their manservant was 10s. 6d., luggage being 8s. 6d. extra. By 1795 these fares had been increased to two insides £2 10s., and one outside 16s. In 1774 Woodforde went from Oxford to Ansford in one day by post-chaises at a cost of £4 8s. for fares, meals, tips and turnpikes. In 1779 Woodforde and his nephew rode from Weston to Ansford, and the six days' journey cost £6 3s. 3½d. When Woodforde passed through London a day or so was spent in seeing the sights, including the Lions of the Tower. He and Nancy stayed at the Bell Savage Inn, on Ludgate Hill, and Woodforde says it was a very good house, but as he was " terribly bit by bugs " we should hardly have agreed with him.

The next stage was by the Salisbury coach, in which two inside places cost £2 2s., one outside 10s. 6d., and luggage 16s. 6d. They left London at ten at night, and got to Salisbury between two and three next afternoon, and then continued their journey by chaises into Somerset. In 1786, when returning from Ansford, they see Mr. Pitt, the Prime Minister, held up at Hindon because all the posting horses were engaged. In 1786 they go there on holiday again and travel by the " Baloon " coach, so called because it was a fast one. Balloons were fashionable and had come over from France, where the first ascent was made by the Montgolfier brothers, paper makers of Annonay, in 1783. The motive power was hot air, generated by a fire in a brazier suspended by chains under an opening at the bottom of the balloon—which sounds fairly hazardous. Woodforde saw his first balloon at Norwich in 1784. Balloons satisfied the feeling which most of us have for something that is fast—that was hardly Nancy's motive, though, for wearing " a neat genteel and pretty Baloon hat."

" Baloon " coaches were possible now that the roads were being improved by the setting up of toll-gates, by making the users of the roads pay for their use and maintenance. We talk of a turnpike road and forget that the name arose from first setting up a frame which turned like a turnstile, with spikes on it to prevent people passing until the toll was paid. For slower traffic and goods there were waggons ; Woodforde in 1793 speaks of meeting a large one with a tilt and drawn by eight horses, as Fig. 31.

BRIDGES.—Improving the old and making new roads turned the attention of the engineers to bridge building— it is an inspiring subject. To throw a bridge across a chasm or overcome the obstacle of a swiftly-flowing river has always tuned up the bridge builders. We see in the " Iliad " how the Greeks thought of a river as something alive : " Nor shall the river avail you anything, fair-flowing with its silver eddies, though long time have you made him sacrifice of many bulls, and thrown down single-hooved horses, still living, into his eddies." The early bridge builders had to watch their rivers in case a sudden flood overwhelmed and whirled them away, still living. It gives us an added respect for the early engineers, who tackled their bridge problems so courageously. Take the Coalbrookdale Bridge, crossing the Severn near Brosely, in Shropshire, as Fig. 71. This was the first cast-iron bridge built, and the circular arch has a span of 100 feet rising 4 feet.

The roads were made by throwing down gravel and stones and depending on the broad-wheeled waggons rolling them into the mud.

SMELTING.—All through the eighteenth century experiments were being made in smelting iron with coal and coke, instead of charcoal as had been the case. As the processes were perfected there was a great change over from counties like Sussex, which used to be a Black Country, to the northern industrial areas, where coal and iron were found together. This brought in its train great alterations in the lives of the people.

STEAM POWER.—But the most momentous change of all was the perfecting of the steam engine by James Watt. When he was a mathematical instrument maker in Glasgow he was asked, in 1763, to repair a model of Newcomen's engine, which gave him many ideas. In 1767 he was trying to make steam engines with Roebuck of Carron ; but Roebuck went bankrupt in 1773, and it was not till 1776 that Watt found the ideal partner in Matthew Boulton of Birmingham, and the steam engine was turned into a success by 1781. One partner could write to the other in 1786 that people were " steam-mill mad." Remember that for thousands of years men had depended on simple

FIG. 71.—The Coalbrookdale Bridge, of Cast Iron, erected 1779.
(Model in Science Museum, London.)

mechanical aids like the lever, and wind, water and their
own muscles, and those of the horse and ox. In steam they
saw endless applications and possibilities. At the end of
the eighteenth century steam was used in sugar, flour and
paper mills, and as we saw on p. 72, Cartwright started
driving his power loom by a steam engine in 1789. In the
textile trades water power had been used before, but it
was steam that really started the modern factory system,
and steam which destroyed the Old England and put
Industrialism in its place.

To see how this came about we shall need to go back a
little. In Vol. II we found out from Celia Fiennes'
description of the serge trade in Exeter that the spinners
brought their yarn to the market and sold it to the weavers,
who in turn sold their cloth to the fullers. The good part
of this system was that, though it did not turn out large
quantities, the quality was good and the industry widespread. The workman could live outside the town in the
country, and his family could assist him. They could if
they felt so disposed take time off to grow their own
vegetables, and keep pigs and poultry. In the same way

they helped to keep the farmer going, because his corn went to the mill and was ground into flour and baked by the village baker into bread. The countryside was not one-sided as it is now, with a solely agricultural population ; life was well-balanced.

The steam engine altered all this, because the operative had to go where the power was, so the factory came into being, and the people were steam-mill mad because they saw that there was money to be made. And a new class came into being—a hard and bitter race, without any culture or tradition behind them. The amenities meant nothing to them ; they even invented a saying : " Where there's muck there's money." How were such a people to solve the tremendous problems with which they were confronted? The country village had a thousand years of tradition behind it as a guide ; the industrial town and factory had none. There had been workshops before, but no factories. When an architect designs a building, unconsciously he draws from his experience—the things he has seen and been taught. When the engineers started designing factories they had no such experience. The actual installation of the central steam engine was simple, but how to distribute the power by shafts, pulleys and belts was a problem. That all had to be invented. Then the lay-out of the looms and the working space necessary for them. The height of the workrooms and the lighting. Water supply probably worried them, and sewage disposal was an awful problem. Then the steam engine itself was inhuman ; it worked continuously, and to make it pay man had to follow its example, and was lucky if he escaped with less than once round the clock on six days of the week. Thus he had to come and live near the mill and leave his garden and his pigs and poultry behind him, so the country-side suffered as well. And there was no superfluity of houses, because the population was increasing. New houses had to be built, and nobody thought of Town Planning.

MEDICINE

A thousand years had gone to make a town before the Industrial Revolution ; during it towns had to be planned at once, and built quickly and cheaply. So back-to-back houses and alleys and slums came into being, and still remain with us. We describe industrial housing on p. 164.

It hardly seems possible that the factory operatives could have been happy. They probably made the best of a bad job ; but compared to the life which is depicted in the Woodforde Diary theirs seems cramped and colourless. The great charm of the Diary is that it gives you the life of the village as well as that of the vicarage. There was poverty at Weston, but much kindliness. There is one delightful entry : " We had a very merry, laughing Day of it," and one feels, as one reads, that there were many such days, and that many participated in them.

One of the greatest of the difficulties of the change over to industrialism was that it came at a time when little was known of the precautions which were necessary to maintain the public health.

MEDICINE.—When we come to the gentle art of healing it does not seem to us an over-statement to say that the fifth-century Greek probably had a better chance of recovery under Hippocrates, who was born 460 B.C., than the people of the early eighteenth century.

The Woodforde Diary is extremely interesting from the point of view of health and medicine. The diarist notes his illnesses and the cures. We find that Dr. Clarke, his brother-in-law, was inoculating in 1764 against small-pox with the virus of the disease itself. Small-pox was the great scourge of the eighteenth century, and pock-marked faces must have been general. The doctors then discovered that, if persons had a slight attack of small-pox, afterwards they were immune, so inoculation was started.

At the end of the eighteenth century they noticed that dairy farmers, who contracted cow-pox, seemed to be protected from small-pox, so Jenner in 1776 introduced vaccination with cow-pox, and this was found to give immunity if the vaccination were repeated at intervals. Jenner, in fact, appears to have been forestalled by a farmer named Jesty. On his tombstone in the churchyard at Worth Matravers, near Swanage, Dorset, is the following inscription : "(Sacred) To the Memory of Benj^m Jesty (of Downshay) who departed this Life April 16th 1816 aged 79 Years. He was born at Yetminster in this County, and was an upright honest Man : particularly noted for having been the first Person (known) that introduced the Cow Pox by Inoculation, and who from his great strength of mind made the Experiment from the (Cow) on his Wife and two Sons in the Year 1774." As the adjoining gravestone of his wife shows that she died in 1824, aged 84, we have proof that she survived her vaccination. The subject is controversial, but the fact remains that a pock-marked face is now uncommon, whereas up till the end of the nineteenth century it was still fairly common.

So far as surgery was concerned, generally this was in the hands of the Barber Surgeons, who were a City company —you could have your hair, corns or throat cut in the same establishment. By 1745 the surgeons had broken away from the barbers, but as the latter kept the funds the first surgeons' society was in great difficulties, until the Royal College of Surgeons was founded in 1800.

John Hunter was one of the first great men to free medicine from quackery and adopt a scientific treatment of disease.

If small-pox was the plague of the land, scurvy was the curse of the sea, but here attempts were made to combat it, and Captain Cook kept his sailors free from the complaint. Lemon juice was one of the preventives.

Fevers were rampant. The wretched prisoners in the gaols, kept there in dirty condition, infected their judges when brought into court (see p. 53). At the Black Assize at the Old Bailey, in London, in April, 1750, the Lord

Fig. 71A.—Dresses for the Seaside.

(Heideloff's Gallery of Fashions.)

Mayor, one of the Justices and forty to fifty others died of typhus fever contracted in this way.

In the Woodforde Diary we read that in 1781 fifty-three people died of fever in one week at Norwich.

The window tax, like all taxes, was bad. It was ingenious and seemed fair, yet it had a bad effect on the public health. It was really taxing by appearances. If you lived in a little Georgian house with a pleasant front door, and a window on each side, and three above, then you did not offer a very easy mark for the vulture tax gatherer; but if you had two or more on each side then the carcass became tempting, and the wretched tax-payer had to pay or brick up his windows. This we find that Woodforde did in 1784, when he had three windows bricked up. Though he saved part of his tax he shut out the sun and fresh air. He paid on the dairy and corn chamber windows as well as the house.

This brings us to another revolution. Until the middle of the nineteenth century the poor consumptive was kept in the warmest and stuffiest conditions, whereas the only chance of recovery for the lung was the fresh-air method which is now employed.

Here are some prescriptions culled from the Woodforde Diary. In 1790 he comes to the conclusion that " near a pint of Port Wine everyday " of the preceding winter was not good for him. It was held to be good to take one hour before breakfast ½ pint of water in which had been steeped the second rind of alder stick. You could be bled 2 ounces, and your horses 2 quarts each. Friars Balsam and " Family Plaister " were used. Rhubarb was the great medicine, and a roasted onion put into your ear cured ear-ache. It was well to have a black tom-cat in your house, because its tail came in handy to rub your eye if you had a stye on the eyelid. A pond in the garden was necessary if there was ague in the house ; the patient was given a dram of gin, pushed headlong into the pond, and then taken out and put to bed. If you had toothache, the farrier, being a handy man, came along and, if he were lucky, drew " the tooth at the first pull." Even the doctors were alarmed if your village was visited by a disorder called " Whirli-gigousticon," as Weston was in 1783. Sea-bathing became fashionable at the end of the eighteenth century, and was one of the best things which ever happened, because the people's bodies were exposed to the sun and air and had a few baths. People went to Bristol Waters, which were held to be a cure for consumption.

In 1793 Woodforde notes that a mad dog ran through his village one day, and that one entry is sufficient to call up what was a constant terror till well towards the end of the nineteenth century. The friendly dog in hot weather was apt to go mad and run slavering at the jaws, biting all he met. Terrible tales were told of the awful death of those who contracted hydrophobia ; how the patients howled and bit like dogs and were thrown into the most fearful convulsions. When there was an epidemic of hydrophobia all the dogs had to be muzzled, and very miserable they looked with wire or leather guards all over their faces, and then a cure was found by Pasteur. This great man, like many others, was led to his discovery in a roundabout way, and began by studying the culture of the vine. If on their death-beds men look back and think of their work, Pasteur could find comfort in the thought that he had saved as many lives as Napoleon sacrificed.

This leads us to the very important subject of our next chapter.

FIG. 72.—The Canal Aqueduct over the Irwell at Barton, Lancashire.

FIG. 73.—Railway Viaduct over the River Medlock and
Ashton Canal, Lancashire.

FIG. 74.—A Passenger Barge to Uxbridge on the Grand
Junction Canal at Paddington, 1801.

FIG. 74A.—Opening the Sluice Gate to raise the level of
the water in the lock, *c.* 1800.

By W. H. Pyne

CHAPTER V

SANITATION

(Chapter dedicated to Venus Cloacina, the Goddess of Sewers.)

NOW here is a chapter which the delicately-minded can skip if they will, because it is concerned with Sanitation—but we hope they will not. Some of the boys and girls who read this book may become doctors, or engineers, or architects, or any one of the occupations which deal with the Public Health, and if they do they must deal with sanitation. It is as well one of the triumphs of the nineteenth century; a lost art was revived and people remembered that cleanliness, and all that it connotes, ranks next to Godliness. The subject has a long history behind it. We saw in our book on Homeric Greece that Sir Arthur Evans found a drainage system at Minoan Cnossos which was carried out in socketed and jointed drain-pipes, and disaster fell on Cnossos as early as 1450 B.C. Fifteenth-century B.C. Cnossos was ahead of eighteenth-century A.D. London so far as sanitation was concerned.

We do not know much of Greek methods of sanitation, but when we come to the Roman there are many evidences. The Romans not only had house drains, but sewers which carried the sewage away. The Cloaca Maxima in Rome can still be traced from the Forum of Nerva to its overflow into the Tiber. This probably started life as a stream, then it was covered with a vault of stone, and had a paved floor of lava added. The Romans even had a goddess of sewers, Venus Cloacina, who was regarded as the Purifier, and it is, when you think a little, a very beautiful idea. To wage war on dirt and disease, to clear away foulness, to make things clean, to purify—is a good work.

BATHS

The Romans brought water to their cities in noble aqueducts, which still remain, here and there, as triumphs of Civil Engineering.

When the Romans came to England in A.D. 43 they brought their ideas of cleanliness with them. We tried to illustrate these in our book on Everyday Life in Roman Britain. At Silchester, which was built in the first century A.D., the public baths there had latrines, where the sewage was carried away by water running through drains. The baths themselves were on a very grand scale for a small provincial town, and were arranged as Turkish baths are to-day, with a series of hot rooms which induce perspiration with a cold plunge to finish off with. Then there was the Great Bath at Bath, with five bathing pools and all kinds of other baths grouped around ; there is nothing comparable to the Roman Bath at Bath in England to-day. Then disaster fell ; Bath was sacked by the Saxons in 577, and its hot pools, lead-lined baths and elaborate system of pipes must have been as incomprehensible to them as a stranded jet-propelled aeroplane would be to-day to the pygmies of the African forests. So the springs choked up and the baths themselves disappeared into a morass. The words of Isaiah on the triumph of Israel over Babylon can be applied to the Roman baths : " I will also make it a possession for the bittern, and pools of water." In the museum at Bath is a teal's egg found when the Baths were excavated in the nineteenth century.

Incredible as it may sound, no real advance was made for 1400 years ; from the early fifth century until the beginning of the nineteenth century people were not concerned with Public Health.

Our Anglo-Saxon ancestors did not like, or understand, city life. Tacitus knew the breed when he wrote : " They live apart, each by himself, as woodside, plain, or fresh spring attracts him." This does not mean single individuals, of course, but families which, with all the uncles and aunts and grandparents, would be like a small tribe, and the spring was the first essential for the English settlements, as it is to-day—if you are building in the country away from Water Companies. Little can be known of sewage disposal until we come to Norman times, and then in all their castles we can find the closets which are called garderobes. These are generally planned with care, and decently tucked into a corner. They are usually approached from a window recess in the thickness of the wall, which acts as a disconnecting lobby, and the garderobes have a narrow slit themselves for ventilation. The actual fitting consists of a stone riser, over which a wooden seat was fixed, and the sewage fell down a vertical stone shaft, discharging into the open at the base of the wall, or in the later castles, into the moat. Garderobes are shown in the plans of castles in " Everyday Things in England," Vol. I. Again the Norman never built his castle until he was sure of the water supply. The well was always in the keep, so that in case of siege the people were sure of water.

The monks in their monasteries seem to have been a little ahead of the citizens in their castles so far as sanitation was concerned. People did bathe in the Middle Ages, because there are frequent illustrations, in the illuminated manuscripts, of them having baths in wooden tubs. Water of course had to be brought in jugs and pails, and poured into the tubs. The Bath has its own order of Chivalry, instituted with us at the Coronation of Henry iv. in 1399. This received its name from the candidates for the honour being put into a bath, on the preceding evening, to denote a purification from evil deeds.

The first mention we have come across of a fitted bath is in Celia Fiennes' Diary, of the time of William and Mary, to which we referred in Vol. II.

But baths like this would only have been for the very grand folks. We do not think there is any mention of a bath in the Woodforde Diary, or of bathing. Woodforde was a charming man—he may, or may not, have bathed.

There was nothing very remarkable about this, because there were many country houses which were still without fitted baths right up to the end of the nineteenth century. A footman or maid brought in a big bath mat first, and then placed on it a large circular tin bath with a rim about 6 inches high, and two cans of water, one hot and the other cold, and in this you sat, or stood, and rinsed off the soap suds as best you could.

Thackeray, who should have known, writing "Pendennis" in the nineteenth century, said, " Gentlemen, there can be but little doubt that your ancestors were the Great Unwashed."

So far as sanitation is concerned the closet was outside in the garden, screened for privacy's sake, and Woodforde refers to it as " Jericho." This was a small outbuilding with a wooden seat, and a pit dug in the ground to receive the sewage. This pit necessarily had to be dug so that it projected at the back of the building for the purpose of cleaning it out. The danger was that surface water could get in, and then percolate through the soil, and so con-taminate the water supply. Water was obtained by sinking a well, and this was the first thing done in building —to sink the well and find out if there were a good water supply. Local knowledge or diviners would be employed. We have several times employed diviners who have found water. Now assuming that in sinking the well the shaft passed through a thin vein of clay, it would be quite possible for sewage seeping through the soil from " Jericho " to be held up by this vein of clay, and then be conducted, if the levels were favourable, to the well. This was the cause of the terrible fevers—tainted water supply. Men, women and children still to-day, unfortunately, live in conditions of dirt and squalor and survive, but if they drink foul water they die, and that speedily and dread-fully. Inside the house, in cases of illness, close-stools, or commodes, were used.

These were the conditions in the country in the

eighteenth century, and, in fact, in remote places they continue still. Granted that the water supply is good, and kept free from contamination, they are tolerable. When, however, as was the case in the eighteenth century, much the same state of affairs ruled in the town, it is easy to see how, when the Industrial Revolution brought many more people to the cities, the conditions soon became intolerable and a grave challenge to public health. We will see what happened in London in the eighteenth century.

In some of the older houses, such as those in Bedford Row, London, no provision was made on the upper floors for any water closet, and originally this office was at the end of the small yard or garden at the back of the house, and it consisted of a privy, or Jericho, which stood over a cesspool. When this needed cleaning out, in many cases the buckets had to be carried through the house. There were cesspools in Red Lion Square and Bedford Row, Holborn, up to 1854. This had to be so because there was no general system of sewers in London. One was constructed in the Strand in 1802, and this probably just ran into the Thames, or down Fleet Street into the Fleet. If you happened to be on the line of a sewer you could connect up to it—otherwise you had to depend on a cesspool. It was not till 1865 that London was provided with a system of main drainage or sewers (p. 106). Even then the difficulties were not over, because it was found as the result of turning the sewage into the streams that a nuisance of a new character was created, as serious as the one which the construction of sewers had relieved.

What house drains there were, were made of brick, in cylindrical form, or with vertical brick sides covered with a stone top as they were in the Middle Ages. Stoneware drain pipes, as used now, were first introduced in 1845, and made by Doultons in 1846. These were jointed with clay up till about 1880, when cement began to be used.

Now for the water supply of London. In Stow's

FIG. 75.—The Well Winch.

"Survey of London" (A.D. 1598) we find that the citizens at first depended on the Thames and its smaller tributaries, like the Fleet and the Walbrooke, and various wells. Water would not have been laid on to the houses, but was fetched by servants from the parish pump. Here and there these still remain, though not in use—there is one at the south end of Bedford Row, London. As the buildings increased these sources began to fail, and water was brought into the city by pipes of lead.

In the sixteenth century a **Dutchman** obtained a lease

from the City of the first arch of London Bridge, on the north side, and put in water wheels which worked pumps that forced the Thames water up to a reservoir, and from thence it was laid on to some of the houses in lead pipes. Pretty foul stuff it must have been, with the incoming tide bringing up garbage from the ships in the pool below the bridge, and the outgoing one sewage from the Fleet.

The New River Company, of which Sir Hugh Myddelton, a goldsmith and citizen of London, was the moving spirit, marked the beginning of the search by great cities for pure water supplies. Springs were discovered near Hertford, twenty miles away, high enough up for the water to run down to London by gravity, and in James I. reign the surveyors got to work, and by 1613 the water flowed into a reservoir at Islington.

Going through Red Lion Square, Holborn, about 1930, we saw some of the old wooden water supply pipes being dug up. These were made of elm trunks, bored out to about 6 inches diameter, and according to Mr. Austin, the Holborn Surveyor, were laid about 1620. Probably at first the water was conducted to pumps at intervals in the streets, and may afterwards have been laid on to storage cisterns in the basements of the houses with lead pipes, and then pumped up to other cisterns to give the head of water for the first water closets which we shall discuss presently. The elm water mains, though very thick, would not have stood a great deal of pressure, and there must have been leakage at the joints ; again, until a proper ball valve was invented, which would shut the valve by its ball rising on the incoming water, the supply must have been regulated by taps ; ball valves are mentioned 1748. The cast lead cisterns which were made in the eighteenth century are very fine, and Fig. 76 shows one. The cistern would not have been cast as a whole, of course, but each side separately, and then soldered together. Sand was spread on the casting table, and then the pattern indented into it from various stock

FIG. 76.—Cast Lead Rain-water Cistern.

pattern moulds and the lead poured on. All sheet lead
was cast in this way, and the pipes were made by cutting
up this cast sheet lead and soldering the joints together,
as was done in Roman Bath. At the beginning of the
nineteenth century lead was rolled out into sheets in
rolling mills, hence it is now called milled lead, and about
1820 lead pipes without any seam began to be drawn
under hydraulic pressure.

In the "London and Country Builders Vade Mecum" of
1748, Section IV., on Plumbers' Work, we find that
"Its usual with the Plumbers to cast their Sheet-Lead of
various Thicknesses, for Guttering, laying of Flats, covering
of Roofs, etc., *viz.* from 7 to 12 lb. the Foot Square ";
to-day we use 5 lb. 7 lb. lead was worth 1*s.* 1½*d.* per foot
and 12 lb. 1*s.* 11*d.* in London. No mention is made in
the book of any work in connection with closets. Rain
water would have been collected from the roofs. This
was made obligatory in London in 1724, for roofs to have
gutters and down pipes. Many other private water
companies were formed after the New River Company
to deal with the growing needs of London, and remained

94

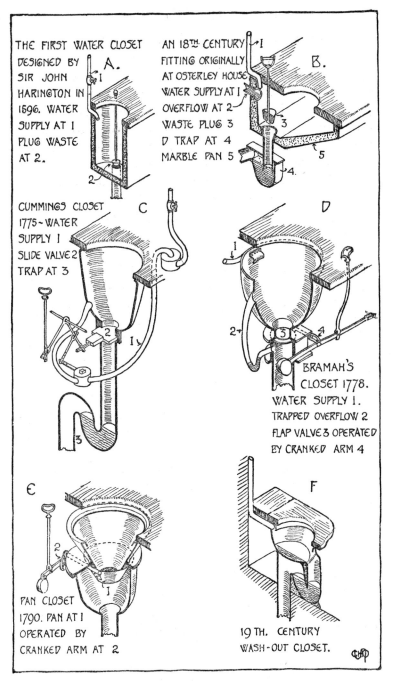

THE FIRST WATER CLOSET DESIGNED BY SIR JOHN HARINGTON IN 1596. WATER SUPPLY AT 1 PLUG WASTE AT 2.

A.

AN 18TH CENTURY FITTING ORIGINALLY AT OSTERLEY HOUSE WATER SUPPLY AT 1 OVERFLOW AT 2 WASTE PLUG 3 D TRAP AT 4 MARBLE PAN 5

B.

CUMMINGS CLOSET 1775 ~ WATER SUPPLY 1 SLIDE VALVE 2 TRAP AT 3

C

D

BRAMAH'S CLOSET 1778. WATER SUPPLY 1. TRAPPED OVERFLOW 2 FLAP VALVE 3 OPERATED BY CRANKED ARM 4

E

PAN CLOSET 1790. PAN AT 1 OPERATED BY CRANKED ARM AT 2

F

19 TH. CENTURY WASH-OUT CLOSET.

FIG. 77.—The Evolution of the Water-Closet.

until 1903, when they were all taken over by the Metropolitan Water Board.

The next detail to be considered is the actual water closet itself, and there is evidence that, though the simple privy in the backyard was quite common in London in the eighteenth century, inventors had been experimenting much earlier than this to improve matters. Sir John Harington is generally credited with being the designer of the first water closet. He did this for use at his home at Kelston, near Bath, and brought out a book about it in 1596. By the use of his closet he claimed that " unsavoury Places may be made sweet, noisome places made wholesome, filthy places made cleanly." A, Fig. 77, has been drawn from the details given in the book. Water was pumped up into a cistern, and then conducted to the pan of the closet and retained there by a valve or plug, which could be pulled up by a handle in the seat. When this was pulled up the sewage was discharged into a cesspool under, and there was no disconnecting trap between the closet or cesspool or any drain.

In Sir John's instructions he says the pan is to be " like the pot of a close-stool," and this is just what his closet was—a close-stool with water laid on, and a plug waste.

The next development came with the type of closet that Mr. S. Stevens Hellyer discovered at Osterley House, of which he wrote in one of his books (1882). He considered it then to be an eighteenth-century fitting. This is B, Fig. 77. It is a valve closet, in that water was kept in the pan by the plug, but it shows an improvement on Sir John Harington's closet, in that sewage was discharged into a lead soil pipe, and this may or may not have been trapped ; it probably was, because of a reference made by Alexander Cumming, a watchmaker of Bond Street, London, who took out the first patent for a water closet in 1775. C, Fig. 77, shows this. In his specification Cumming claimed, as advantages for his closet, the shape of the pan, the manner of admitting water, and that the stink trap was of an improved shape which totally emptied itself each time the closet was used. He then goes on to state that hitherto, though the stink trap had cut off the smell of the drains, it was offensive in itself because it became " a magazine of fœtid matter."

W.C.'s were beginning to be fitted inside houses, and are shown on plans of 1775, and very dangerous they proved to be. The apparatus was held to be so magical that all you had to do was put it in under the stairs, with or without a window, take an unventilated pipe to a cesspool, and live happy ever after. Instead, you very frequently died, because foul gases were conducted into the house.

The question of traps which cut off the stink had better be dealt with now. The vertical pipe below the trap in C, Fig. 77, was taken down to the ground level, and as often as not inside the house—there it was connected up to the drains which went to the cesspool. There was no fresh air inlet to the drains, or ventilator to the soil pipe as shown in Fig. 78; so traps were invented to cut off the smell. The first patent for a stink-trap seems to have been taken out by John Gaillait, a cook, in 1782, for "the invention of an entire new machine a stink-trap, . . . which will entirely prevent the very disagreeable smells from drains and sewers." At first these were made up by the plumber, out of sheet lead soldered together, in the form shown on B, Fig. 77; because of their shape they were called D traps. It is also quite obvious that they were not self-cleansing, and that Cumming's trap, as shown in C, Fig. 77, was a very much better type. The valve in Cumming's closet took the form of a slide.

The next development came when Joseph Bramah, a cabinet maker, took out a patent, in 1778, for another form of valve closet. This is shown in D, Fig. 77. The basin is the same shape as Cumming's—the difference was in the arrangement of the valve. This was hinged on its side and by a cranked arm was shut up against the bottom

THE SEWER IS CUT OFF BY AN INTERCEPTING TRAP AT A WITH A CLEANING BRANCH FROM MANHOLE B WHERE DRAINS CAN BE INSPECTED UNTIL FRESH AIR GOES IN AT C AND PASSES UP SOIL PIPE D WHICH ACTS AS THE MAIN VENTILATING PIPE. THE SOIL PIPE ONLY TAKES SEWAGE FROM W.C.s WHICH ARE CONNECTED TO IT BY BRANCHES AS AT E. EACH W.C. IS TRAPPED & THE LOWER W.C.s PROVIDED WITH ANTI-SYPHONAGE PIPES AS AT F SO THAT WHEN AN UPPER W.C. IS DISCHARGED THE WATER IS NOT SYPHONED OUT OF THE TRAPS OF THE LOWER W.C.s WASTE FROM BATHS LAV. BASINS & SINKS ARE TAKEN TO A SEPARATE PIPE. WITH TRAPPED BRANCHES SYPHONAGE IS PREVENTED BY PUFF PIPES AS AT G. TAKEN TO THE OUTER FACE OF WALL. SOIL & WASTE PIPES ARE KEPT ON OUTSIDE OF WALL.

COVER
REMOVED

FIG. 78.—The English Two-pipe System of Drainage.

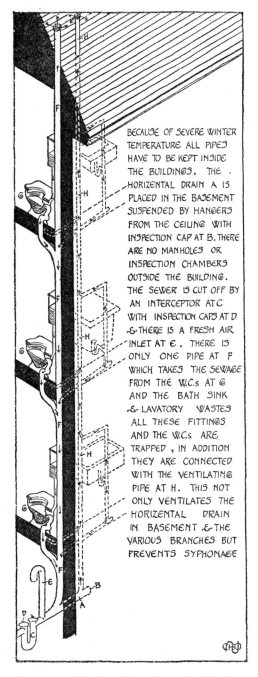

BECAUSE OF SEVERE WINTER TEMPERATURE ALL PIPES HAVE TO BE KEPT INSIDE THE BUILDINGS. THE HORIZENTAL DRAIN A IS PLACED IN THE BASEMENT SUSPENDED BY HANGERS FROM THE CEILING WITH INSPECTION CAP AT B. THERE ARE NO MANHOLES OR INSPECTION CHAMBERS OUTSIDE THE BUILDING. THE SEWER IS CUT OFF BY AN INTERCEPTOR AT C WITH INSPECTION CAPS AT D & THERE IS A FRESH AIR INLET AT E. THERE IS ONLY ONE PIPE AT F WHICH TAKES THE SEWAGE FROM THE W.C.s AT G AND THE BATH SINK & LAVATORY WASTES ALL THESE FITTINGS AND THE W.C.s ARE TRAPPED, IN ADDITION THEY ARE CONNECTED WITH THE VENTILATING PIPE AT H. THIS NOT ONLY VENTILATES THE HORIZENTAL DRAIN IN BASEMENT & THE VARIOUS BRANCHES BUT PREVENTS SYPHONAGE

FIG. 79.—The American One-pipe System.

of the basin. Bramah's principle is still retained in such modern valve closets as the " Optimus." The difficulty about all valve closets is that they must be well made and so are expensive.

The pan closet dates from the end of the eighteenth century (1790) and, being simpler to make, was cheaper, but the container under, as shown in E, Fig. 77, was much too large to be cleansed by the flush, and so it was a very offensive type. Still it continued in use until 1881, because it was condemned by Mr. Hellyer in his lectures given in that year.

Wash-out closets were another bad nineteenth-century type, and are shown in F, Fig. 77—they failed because they were not self-cleansing. Still they led the way to the modern pedestal wash-down type as shown in Fig. 78.

Having said as much as is necessary about the fittings, we can turn to the drains. We will begin with the things which should be avoided first. It is useless to put good fittings on to bad drains. One of the authors remembers being called in, as late as 1913, to advise a doctor who was retiring and had bought a lovely old house in Kent without having the drains tested. There were good modern water closets which were visible—everything else was invisible. The oldest inhabitant assured us that the sewage was taken to a cesspool in the garden, but as there were no inspection chambers, or visible soil pipes, or any fresh air inlets, or means of ventilating the drains, this statement was not taken on trust. Exploration was put in hand, and the vertical soil pipe from the W.C.'s was discovered buried in the wall descending to the ground level. Here it was connected to stoneware drains which ran about on the surface of the ground under the wooden floors inside the house. Straight pipes had been used to get round curves, so that the flanged joints, of course, were well open on the outside of the curve. It was a terrible spectacle—yet people had lived in the house, on the top of sewage continually seeping into the soil under it.

This, of course, was a survival of a state of affairs which had been general in the nineteenth century. It was in 1871 that King Edward VII., who was then Prince of Wales, caught typhoid fever when staying at a house in Yorkshire. This was traced to bad drainage; so even Princes were not immune from danger. The Prince's illness served, however, to focus public attention on the matter, and a group of men which included Edwin Chadwick, Professor W. H. Corfield, Rogers Field and S. Stevens Hellyer evolved the modern system of sanitation. Hellyer, being the head of a plumbing firm which had been established in London since 1706, was enabled to put the principles into practice, and he it was who gave a series of lectures at the Society of Arts in 1881, and published them in book form in 1882. Fig. 78 can be taken as illustrating the result of the work that these men did. The details to be noted are that though the drains are cut off by traps, there are not nearly so many stink-traps as there used to be, because the drains themselves are ventilated.

The scheme shown in Fig. 78 seems so simple that one's first impression is that it is so ordinary that it calls for no remark at all—yet it took a long time to come about. Mr. Norman Shaw, the well-known architect of the nineteenth century, fixed valve closets without any traps under the fitting, and took a branch drain into an open head on the top of the soil pipe. This was not carried up, so any unpleasant smell was free to escape from this head, and be carried by draught into any adjacent open window. The fresh air inlet was at the foot of the soil pipe, and this was trapped beyond just under the ground level. This was in 1878.

The end of the nineteenth century was a great time for English plumbers, and it can be said quite safely that for some time then they led the way and plumbed the whole world—but this success led to rigid bye-laws which have since blocked the way to progress. Fig. 78 will show that we still regard drainage as a foul thing which is going to stink, and this must be kept outside the house. There seems also behind it the idea the English are a dirty, careless race, who cannot be trusted to keep themselves clean and decent without fool-proof apparatus and constant inspection. This may be typical of the official mind, but it is a gross libel, for with little exception the reverse is the case. The exterior pipes get stopped and often cracked during even a moderate frost, and a long spell of our old severe weather would cause dislocation of drainage and possibly a nasty epidemic. The system involves the provision of very expensive drainage laid in the ground, with all the apparatus of inspection chambers and so on ; yet the soil pipes above the ground are of iron jointed in lead, and as they are tested by being plugged at the bottom, and filled with water, they are watertight and airtight. Outside the house they give the appearance of varicose veins, and are very unsightly. Connecting the ground floor W.C. directly to the manhole as shown in Fig. 78 is bad practice, because it is unventilated. The outside gullies, too, attract rats.

Fig. 79 shows the American one-pipe system, and the notes on the side explain how it was developed by the severe weather conditions. It is at once obvious that it is a cheaper and better system than the English two-pipe one.

Here only one set of pipes is shown—but if you bear in mind that in addition there are those which supply hot and cold water to the fittings—the heating pipes—those which carry wires for electric light and bells—others for refrigeration and so on, you will get some idea of what a complicated organism a modern building is, especially if, as is the case in the Empire State Building of New York, there are eighty-two storeys—that the building is about 1250 feet high, and houses round about 30,000 people.

That is perhaps all we need say about Sanitation, but it will be sufficient to show what an awful problem confronted the civic authorities during the Industrial

FIG. 80.—Death, the Avenger.

(The outbreak of cholera at a Masked ball in Paris in 1831.)

FIG. 80A.—The South Drawing Room, showing some of the "Dolphin" Furniture made in 1813 in commemoration of Nelson, belonging to the Admiralty.

FIG. 80B.—The Banqueting Room (see Frontispiece) showing the Table laid with Contemporary Appointments for a Banquet of 24 Guests.

THE ROYAL PAVILION, BRIGHTON.

FIG. 80c.—Monmouth Street, Soho, an illustration by G. Cruikshank
for Dickens' " Sketches by Boz."

K

Revolution. Here are some notes on plumbers' wages taken from Mr. Bertram Hellyer's book. In 1837 plumbers worked nine hours a day for 6d. an hour, and six full days in the week, which made their wages 27s.—by 1844 they were getting 5s. a day—1854, 5s. 6d. a day—in 1855 they started leaving off work at four o'clock on Saturday instead of 5.30—from 1861-1873 6s. 4d. a day was paid and the Saturday half-holiday started at one o'clock.

There is one other point to be borne in mind, and that is the clearance of dust and garbage in modern cities. Our dustbins are emptied and that is all we know about it —but our ancestors were not so fortunate. Here is a quotation from a letter in the London Times of February 15th, 1832, only just over 100 years ago, " As the cholera is in London, I beg to call your attention to some parts of Westminster, which, above all other places, is the most probable to furnish fuel to the contagion. The Almonry, near Westminster-abbey, is inhabited by the very scum of society : it is unpaved, and the receptacle of all sorts of rubbish. This street has long been a disgrace to the City of Westminster, and the attention of the Board of Health ought to be directed to it, and also to Duck-lane, Pie-street, Cathead Lane, Gardener's Lane, and Stratton-ground, all of them filthy places, where refuse of vegetables rotting and corrupting lies in the streets, contaminating the air, and affording a repast to a herd of swine, which are continually to be seen in those disgusting dens." Perhaps we can get some slight idea of such conditons from the illustration (Fig. 80c), of one of the vanished rookeries in Soho. Notice the wizened brats sailing boats and making-believe to fish in the gutter, and the woman and baby emerging from their trap-door cellar. But the artist cannot reproduce the smells !

Defective and primitive conditions still largely obtain in some of the continental cities, and explain why, in a country like France, with a higher birth-rate, the death-rate is higher than in England, so that the population does not show even the same slight rate of increase as in this island. Toulon is a charming old picturesque city to visit, but its little narrow side-streets are full of heaps of garbage, which at night are rummaged over by the starveling cats. You find much the same state of affairs if you pay a visit to Corsica.

Fig. 80 shows that Death was the Avenger, and death always stalks a little behind, and is only kept at bay by the work of men like those we have mentioned ; wherefore we say this chapter has been worth writing and reading.

An extraordinary thing is that we searched the metropolis for a memorial to the men who won the fight against dirt and disease, a greater battle than many of those which are commemorated by statues of generals. We may say that the whole town in its cleanliness is their best memorial. It almost seemed as if there was nothing at all, until at last we found on the Victoria Embankment a bronze roundel containing a bust, with flowing moustache and whiskers, of Sir Joseph Bazalgette, the Civil Engineer. He was the man to carry out the great scheme of the main drainage of London, by which the sewage of the whole vast metropolis is collected and finds its outlet in a great sewer into the Thames at Barking. But few of the myriad workers of London who go backwards and forwards by the trams along the Embankment realize what they owe to him who is commemorated in this modest fashion, or how frightful were the conditions before the drainage of London was thus carried away and rendered harmless. Mr. Batsford tells us that as a boy he saw a copy of the classic paper read by Bazalgette before the Institution of Civil Engineers on the main drainage of London, extracted from their Transactions.

The way the one great central drainage system of London came into being is a remarkable story and covers a good many years of the middle of the nineteenth Century. There were all sorts of Commissions and schemes, but nothing was done because all the suggestions got thrown out by Boards or Government Departments who had the right of veto. At last in 1855 the Metropolitan Board of Works was constituted and Bazalgette became Chief Engineer. Still controversies caused endless delay until Disraeli passed a short Act in 1858 which gave the Board full control. The fight had gone on for ten years, but now the designs could be put in hand and contracts let, and in 1865 the main drainage was opened by Edward, Prince of Wales, though the whole work was not finished for another ten years. It certainly is on a metropolitan scale. Even in those days more than eighty-three miles of large inter-secting sewers were constructed; over 100 square miles, comprising a vast population, was drained, with a daily discharge of 120 million gallons; the total works cost £4,600,000. There was still one more Commission to be appointed (1882–1884), but that reported strongly in favour of the scheme, and praised the engineering genius which Bazalgette had put forth " in carrying it through all the intricate difficulties of its construction," with remarkable results in improving the general health of London's people.

It is appropriate that Bazalgette's monument should commemorate him on the Embankment, because at the same time as he was working on the draining scheme, he carried through the complicated construction of the Victoria Embankment and later the Albert and Chelsea Embank-ments, with Northumberland Avenue, at a total cost of £2,150,000.

Bazalgette also carried out alterations to many of the old bridges and designed new ones at Putney and Battersea, with the steam ferry at Woolwich.

He remained the Chief Engineer to the Metropolitan Board of Works until it was merged in the London County Council in 1889, and he presented in all thirty-three Annual Reports setting forth the engineering work on which he had been engaged.

PART II

CHAPTER VI

THE NINETEENTH-CENTURY FARMER

IN more ways than one, the perfecting of James Watt's steam engine in 1781 marked the close of one epoch and the beginning of another. In the same year, on October 19th, Cornwallis surrendered at Yorktown, and the American Colonies, almost against the wish of the colonists, were lost to us. The discontent had been simmering since the Stamp Act of 1765, and boiling point was reached at the Boston Tea Party of 1773—hostilities started at Lexington in 1775, and the Declaration of Independence followed (July 4th, 1776). The noble opening preamble of this : " We hold these truths to be self-evident : —That all men are created equal ; that they are endowed by their Creator with certain unalienable rights ; that among these are life, liberty, and the pursuit of happiness," is indicative of much. When Thomas Jefferson of Virginia drew this up he felt life, liberty and happiness were endangered. Thirteen years later the citizens of a much older civilization felt the same, and it was overthrown to the cry of Liberty, Equality and Fraternity, and from the French Revolution Buonaparte was to arise and threaten Europe. The pursuit of happiness became terribly difficult.

We were to go to war with France, and this was to last till 1815 and include another war with America, in 1812. Political history is not in our line of country at all but it must, at this period, be borne in mind. George III. and his advisers, and the Regent, had a fearful task pre-

107

CHART II.

Kings, Political, and Social		Science and Industry		Art	
	GEORGE III. (contd.)	1800	Royal Coll. of Surgeons founded	1800–12	Elgin Marbles come to Lond
1801	Victory at Copenhagen	1801	"Charlotte Dundas," steamboat Trevithick's steam carriage		
1802	Peace of Amiens	1802	Sewer constructed in the Strand Bodley Range	1802	Pitzhanger House, Ealing (Soan
1803	War against Buonaparte			1803	Sheraton's Cabinet Dictionary
1804		1804	Jacquard's apparatus Trevithick's first railway loco.		
1805	Battle of Trafalgar			1805–15	Scott's Romantic Poems
				1806–13	Ashridge, Herts (Wyatt)
1807	Abolition of slave trade Population of England and Wales 11,000,000			1807	Downing Coll., Cambs. (Wilkin
1808		1808	Trevithick's "Catch-me-who-can"	1808	Ackermann's "Microcosm"
				1809	Tavistock Square (London)
1810	Cobbett imprisoned				
1811	Prince of Wales becomes Regent The Luddites			1811	Dulwich Picture Gallery (Soan
				1811–14	C. R. Cockerell in Greece
1812	War with America	1812	Birth of A. W. N. Pugin George Stephenson at Killingworth		Regent St., London (Nash)
1814				1814	Scott's Waverley Novels begun
1815	Battle of Waterloo Corn Law	1815	Steamers on the Thames	1815–23	Shelley, Keats and Byr writing
1816				1816	British Museum buy Elgin Mart
				1817	Waterloo Bridge, London (Renr Customs House, London
1818			Hobby horse introduced		
1819	Peterloo massacre			1819	St. Pancras Ch., London (Inwoo Menai Bridge (Telford)
1820	GEORGE IV			1820	Brighton Pavilion completed (N
1821	Cobbett begins his Rides				
		1822	George Stephenson goes to Stockton and Darlington Rly.		
1823	Cornfields at Earl's Court, London			1823	British Museum, London (Smir
1825				1825	London Bridge
1826			Patrick Bell's reaper		
1827				1827	Carlton House Terrace, Londo University Coll., London (Wilki (cast-iron girders used)
1828	Arnold at Rugby, 1828–42				
1829	"Peelers" make first patrol	1829	Shillibeer's bus Rainhill trials won by "Rocket"		
1830	WILLIAM IV				
1831			Faraday discovers electro-magnetic induction		
1832	Reform Bill				
1833	Oxford Movement Abolition of Colonial slavery	1833	Death of Trevithick Cholera in London Enterprising Steam Coach	1833	National Gallery, London (Wilk
1834	National education begun	1834	Hansom designs his cab McCormick's reaper	1834	Fishmongers' Hall, London (Rober
1835					
1836			Birth of Mrs. Beeton (her book 1859–63)	1836	"The Pickwick Papers" (Dicke
1837	VICTORIA		P. & O founded	1837	Carlyle's "History of Fre Revolution"
		1838	Lord Brougham's brougham	1838	Britten and Pugin's "Public Bu ings"
1839		1839	First bicycle	1839	Harvey Lonsdale Elmes wins co petition for St. George's H Liverpool
					Taylor and Randolph Buildin Oxford (C. R. Cockerell)
1840				1840	Houses of Parliament, Westmin
1841					
		1842	Royal Commission of Mines found that women pulled the coal trucks on hands and feet, and children of five worked alone in the darkness		
1843					
1845		1845	Stoneware drainpipes introduced Howe invents lock-stitch machine		
				1846	Thackeray begins "Vanity Fair"
				1846–47	Cockerell finishes Basevi's F william Museum, Cambri
1847				1847	Elmes dies and Cockerell finis St. George's Hall, Liverpool The end of traditional architec
1849				1848	Macaulay's "History of Englar
1851			Great Exhibition, London		"Jane Eyre" (Charlotte Bron
		1864	London sewerage system		

Chart I.—George II and III, 1727-1799, p.xiv.

sented to them at a time when the whole social and economic structure was being rebuilt.

NINETEENTH-CENTURY FARMING.—The closing years of the eighteenth, and the beginning of the nineteenth century, found farming in a difficult and unreal position. The War was on, and prices had risen to famine heights. The Woodforde Diary is very interesting in this respect. Wheat sent in to Norwich from Weston sold for anything between 47s. and 54s. a quarter between 1784 and 1794. In 1795 and '96 it was 84s. and 105s. In 1797 44s. In 1800 and 1801 114s. to 160s. This was thoroughly bad, because the money which the farmers were making came out of the pockets of the community, and the poor suffered. 1795 was a very cold winter, and £46 15s. was collected in Weston for the poor people, and there was mobbing at Norwich because of the dearness of provisions. Woodforde and Nancy on their way back from their holiday stayed in London to see the opening of Parliament, and got mixed up with a violent mob which broke the windows of the King's Coach, and insulted him, and cried out, " Give us Peace and Bread!" There were riots again in London in 1796. It was this year that Woodforde went to a dinner party where the bread served had been made of all brown wheat meal, with one part in four of barley flour added. Woodforde said of this it " eat very well indeed, may we never eat worse." In this year he instances the following food prices as very high indeed. Beef $6\frac{1}{2}d$. per lb., Mutton 6d., Lamb 6d., Veal 5d., Honey 6d. lb. In 1799 bread was being distributed to the poor in Weston, and in 1801 the Diary complains of high prices and no sign of Peace ; a 6d. loaf sold for 17d., and the poor stole turnips to stay their hunger ; there were mobs and risings, and wages were not increased. Woodforde still paid Ben Leggatt £10, Bretingham Scurl £8, Betty Dade £5 5s., Sally Gunton £5 5s., and the skip-jack £2 2s. per annum.

This led to one of the most disastrous steps ever taken in English history. In May, 1795, the magistrates met at

Speenhamland, New-
bury, Berks, and
there they agreed to
raise the labourer's
wages to 3s. a week
for himself, and 1s. 6d.
a week for the other
members of his family,
when the loaf cost a
shilling, by payments
from the parish rates
—if the loaf increased
so did the dole.
This gradually spread
through most of the
counties, and pauper-
ized the labourers.
The enclosures had cut
them off the land.
Pitt's Combination
Acts of 1799 prevented
any combinations of
workmen who might

FIG. 81.—Milkman with Yoke.

wish to meet to discuss their grievances. Poaching was a
dangerous form of pot-hunting, because you could be transported if found carrying a net, and man-traps and spring
guns were used until 1827.

Probably Nelson's victory at Copenhagen on April 2nd,
1801, when he turned his blind eye to Hyde Parker's signal
to leave off action, saved England in more ways than one.
It put an end to the armed neutrality, and opened the
Baltic to trade, and enabled us to import corn. The Peace
of Amiens led to a short cessation of the War. Corn at
Norwich fell to 76s. a quarter.

The main reason for all this trouble in England was fear.
The authorities had before them the spectacle of the French
Revolution leading to the execution of Louis XVI. in 1793.

They feared revolution at home—they feared invasion by the French. They had to carry on a war while the whole economic structure of the country was being changed. There was no time for kindly inquiry, and repression took its place, with the result that we had labour troubles during the nineteenth century which could have been avoided if the workers had felt that they had been given a fair deal.

War was declared against Buonaparte in 1803 and continued until the bogey was finally laid at Waterloo in 1815. Now here is a point to be remembered. We are apt to think that no other war made such demands on the manhood of the nation as the War of 1914-1918. Sir John Fortescue, the very distinguished military historian, in *The Times* of July 30th, 1932, wrote : " I am not so sure of that. Between 1804 and 1814 the proportion of men under arms, afloat and ashore, to the total population of Great Britain, was exactly the same as in the last war, one in fourteen." In 1914 the industrial machine was at its highest state of efficiency—in 1804 Industrialism was producing muddle and confusion.

After Waterloo the Corn Law of 1815 prevented importation of corn until the price was 80s. a quarter. This was passed by members who represented the agricultural interests—it went against those of the industrial towns who wanted cheap food, but places like Manchester and Birmingham were unrepresented.

Bearing these details in mind we can turn to Cobbett, because, if Tull is the first name which comes to one's mind when writing of farming in the eighteenth century, then William Cobbett's does the same thing when the early nineteenth century is being dealt with.

Cobbett commenced his Rides on October 30th, 1821, when he was fifty-nine years old. His object was to talk to all the people he could meet and try and find a solution of their troubles. He was born at Farnham, in Surrey, on March 9th, 1762, and his father was a small farmer. Cobbett's boyhood was passed in scaring birds from

FIG. 82.—The Bailiff.

growing crops, until, in the end, he was promoted to driving a team and ploughing. His father, who was a man of parts, taught his sons the three R's of Reading, Writing and Arithmetic in the winter evenings, and this carried William through.

When he was eleven he went off with $6\frac{1}{2}d$. in his pocket to see the Royal Gardens of Kew, where he obtained work, and then later returned to Farnham. At Kew he read the " Tale of a Tub." In 1782 he went to Portsdown Hill to visit a relative, and saw the sea for the first time. Here he tried to become a sailor, but was dissuaded. In 1783 he found his way to London, and took a job as a clerk in a lawyer's office in Gray's Inn for some nine months. Then he went to Chatham, and enlisted in the 54th Foot Regiment—for some twelve months he stayed there learning his drill. Here it was that, finding his grammar shaky, he bought a Louth's Grammar, and memorized the whole book, repeating it to himself when on duty as a sentry.

Cobbett did his duty well, and became a good soldier, and finished as sergeant-major. The regiment was sent to Nova Scotia, and Cobbett remained there until 1791, when he obtained his discharge and returned to England. In 1792 he was in France, but in October of that year back in America, this time in Philadelphia, where he taught English to French refugees. By 1795 Cobbett was writing pamphlets, and brought out a monthly political paper called *Peter Porcupine.* This was aptly named, and an action for libel compelled Cobbett to return to England in 1800. Cobbett, of course, could not keep out of a row. Feelings at the time were very high between the Federalists and Republicans, and the rule of the former came to an end with the election of Jefferson to the Presidency. When Cobbett got home he was at first kindly received by the supporters of the Government, and this is interesting, because afterwards he was to be persecuted and prosecuted and imprisoned, and was thought of as a dangerous scribbler who wished to overthrow established government. This was entirely wrong; Cobbett loved his country with a great and abiding love, but it was the country rather than the town.

He would have agreed with Socrates' quotation in Xenophon's Œconomicus that " agriculture to be the mother and nurse of other arts ; for when agriculture flourishes, all other pursuits are in full vigour ; but when the ground is forced to lie barren, other occupations are almost stopped."

By 1802 Cobbett was publishing his *Political Register* (which lasted till his death in 1835). In a year or so he was able to take a house in Botley in Hampshire, and here he grew many trees. He was always extolling the virtues of the Locust, or Acacia tree, which he imported from America. He carried on his farming on the Tullian principles of planting by drills in rows.

Then in 1809 a mutiny broke out among the local militia at Ely, and was suppressed by German cavalry, and the ringleaders sentenced to 500 lashes each. In the *Political Register*, Cobbett remarked on the brutality of the punishment, and described what such a flogging meant. Again he was prosecuted for libel, and sentenced in 1810 to two years' imprisonment, and a fine of £1000. In Cobbett's own words, he " was put into a place among felons (Newgate), from which I had to rescue myself, at the price of twelve guineas a week "—the gaolers were entitled to make a profit in this way. His enemies thought

FIG. 83.—A Leather-Legged Chap.

that they had ruined him, but the *Register* was written in prison, and published regularly, and a book as well on " Paper against Gold."

Cobbett was prosecuted once more for libel in 1831, but was acquitted.

After the War was over the situation was further complicated by the returning soldiers, by unemployment, and intolerable taxation. The people felt Reform was needed, but had no real voice where rotten boroughs and villages returned members to Parliament. Statesmen were not honest—peculation was rampant—even the parsons were pluralists who collected livings, and the tithes, and farmed them out to curates without influence. Into this nightmare world of 1812 came Cobbett, fresh from, and refreshed by gaol, more of a porcupine than ever, and determined to smash what he called the THING; he spoke of it as if it were unclean, and hated all the people who had lent money to the Government to prosecute the War, because they had lent the money when wheat was three times the price that it came to be after, so they were called Fund Lords—stockjobbers he detested because they gambled in War Loan—he described them as " huckstering reptiles who had amassed money by watching the turn of the market "—and bankers because they manipulated currency. Here is what he said of an M.P. who absented himself from Westminster, " He must turn-to or turn-out : he is a sore to Westminster ; a set-fast on its back ; a cholic in its belly ; a cramp in its limbs ; a gag in its mouth : he is a nuisance ; a monstrous nuisance, in Westminster, and he must be abated," and he had never a good word for the parsons, but he loved the village labourer, and pointed out how hard his lot was, and that he was paid so little in wages, that he was worse off for food than the felon in gaol —and he hated London, which he called the Wen, because it drew all the goodness out of the country.

Cobbett loved the old " resident native gentry, attached to the soil, known to every farmer and labourer from their childhood, frequently mixing with them in those pursuits where all artificial distinctions are lost, practising hospitality without ceremony from habit and not in calculation " —he loved these people because they knew their job, but foresaw that they would disappear under the load of taxation, and their place be taken by profiteers. It was for these latter that he reserved the lash of his tongue.

Here was a pretty kettle of fish. Cobbett was no mere vulgar agitator to be bought off by some little preferment— he was entirely honest, and a lover of England, and all he wanted was to make it a better place to live in by Parliamentary Reform. He might have been all this, and yet not have achieved so much, but for the fact that the gods, knowing that he was to have a hardish life, dropped a little magic into his cup and gave him the power to move men ; he was a poet as well as a political propagandist. So his enemies are forgotten and his name lives.

By 1817 Cobbett had to go to America once more— publish his *Register* there, and send it to England. In this way he defeated the Government who were trying to stifle the demand for Reform by the Gagging Bills. Cobbett was a great warrior in the fight that was waged then for the Freedom of the Press.

Cobbett returned in 1819, and by 1821 had started his Rural Rides. He entered Parliament in 1832, in the days of the Reform Bill.

Now for some details of everyday life culled from

FIG. 84.—Sowing Broadcast.

Cobbett's pages. On November 20th, 1821, he goes in pilgrimage to the farm of Tull at Shalbourne, Berks (see p. 10). He goes again later, and many times he acknowledges his debt to Tull's teaching.

He suggests that the labourers in the woodlands and clays of the Weald did better for themselves than in the rich cornlands. He describes them as " leather - legged chaps "—their dress was as follows : " Under the sole of the shoe is iron : from the sole six inches upwards is a high-low ; then comes a leather bam to the knee ; then comes a pair of leather breeches ; then comes a stout doublet ; over this comes a smock-frock ; and the wearer sets brush, and stubs, and thorns, and mire, at defiance." What Cobbett meant, of course, was that woodlands provide pleasant and profitable work for the winter in cutting hop-poles, faggots, and the like, and as well the labourer was sure of firing for himself.

Commons and wastes gave the opportunity for raising geese. Cobbett wrote, " I have seen not less than 10,000 geese in one tract of common, in about 6 miles, going from Chobham towards Farnham in Surrey." This sensible habit of keeping geese on the commons lasted until the last few years in our part of the country, and was a very economical method of raising food. The geese were turned out in the morning to find their own living, and the attendant gander protected them during the day and brought them back at night.

Now we can give the other side of Cobbett. In reading " Rural Rides " his denunciations of stock-jobbers do become a little tiresome, though from his point of view these were good journalism. It was necessary for him to keep on saying the same thing until he established his point, but the jolly part of his books is that you never know when he may forget his enemies and write of the country he loved.

Here is a beautiful description of woodlands :

" Woodland countries are interesting on many accounts. Not so much on account of their masses of green leaves, as on account of the variety of sights, and sounds, and incidents, that they afford. Even in winter, the coppices are beautiful to the eye, while they comfort the mind, with the idea of shelter and warmth. In spring, they change their hue from day to day, during two whole months, which is about the time from the first appearance of the delicate leaves of the birch, to the full expansion of those of the ash ; and, even before the leaves come at all to intercept the view, what, in the vegetable creation, is so delightful to behold, as the bed of a coppice bespangled with primroses and blue-bells ? The opening of the birch leaves, is the signal for the pheasant to begin to crow, for the blackbird to whistle, and the thrush to sing ; and, just when the oak-buds begin to look reddish, and not a day before, the whole tribe of finches burst forth in songs from every bough, while the lark, imitating them all, carries the joyous sounds to the sky. These are amongst the means which Providence has benignantly appointed to sweeten the toils by which food and raiment are produced ; these the English Plough-man could once hear, without the sorrowful reflection that

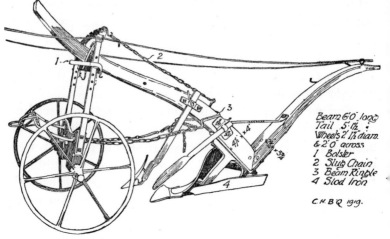

Beam 6'0" long
Tail 5' 1½;
Wheels 2' 1½ diam.
& 2'0 across
1 Bolster
2 Slud Chain
3 Beam Ringle
4 Slod Iron

C.H.B.Q. 1919.

FIG. 85.—Old Plough at Hemsby, Norfolk.

he himself was a *pauper*, and that the bounties of nature had, for him, been scattered in vain ! "

Then Cobbett gets on to his cob again, and begins to lay around him with prodigious thwack, thwacks, at taxation, and accursed paper money—but one can put up with this if, in between, are pieces of prose as pure as the one we have quoted.

And there are many others. Cobbett had an extraordinarily keen eye for a bit of country, when he goes north he notices the difference between north and south. He had a way of judging a district by the number of churches. Where in the south, in a fertile valley, he comes on a church every two miles or so, then he thinks the land was good, and must have supported a large population in the Middle Ages when the churches were built. In the north, from Morpeth to Alnwick, he remarks that the land is poor, scarcely any trees, " the farms enormously extensive ; only two churches, I think, in the whole twenty miles." Cobbett made the following comparison ; Northumberland, with an area of 1871 square miles, had 88 parishes, while Suffolk, with 1512 square miles, had 510, and how rules for one part of the country could not be applied to another.

WHEAT

Then he is distressed not to find many birds in Lincoln-shire. He says, "We heard a little twittering from one thrush ; but, at that very moment, if we had been as near to just such a wood in Surrey, or Hampshire, or Sussex, or Kent, we should have heard ten thousand birds singing altogether, and the thrushes continuing their song till twenty minutes after sunset."

Cobbett tells an amusing lark tale, which we have never seen enacted ourselves. He watched a gentleman lark circling upwards and singing gloriously—then from close by, straight up to him, went the lady lark and obviously gave him a lecture, because the poor songster stopped and flew down to earth. Cobbett suggests that the lady said to her husband, " Yes, my boy, we all know that you have got a very nice voice, but singing won't feed the family "—but then larks sing long before any family comes.

Though Cobbett loved old churches, and the delights of the countryside, his main concern was agriculture, and the condition of the labourers. For example, in his ride to Huntingdon, in 1822, he notes that he did not see any wheat drilled, but that they still persisted in sowing broadcast (Fig. 84), and that so badly that some parts of the field looked as if the seed had been " flung along them with a shovel, while other parts contained only here and there a blade."

At Burghclere, Hants, Cobbett saw a crop of wheat planted in the Tullian manner, in rows, on ridges, at wide intervals, and ploughed, or hoed, in between all the summer. The crop equalled 28 bushels to the acre. Another wheat crop was dibbled in between rows of turnips, in November, four rows on a ridge, with 18 inches between each two rows, and a 5-foot interval between the outside rows. So in Cobbett's time wheat was still sewn broadcast, dibbled, and drilled. Again in the Cotswolds he found ploughing done by oxen. Fig. 100, from J. F. Herring's picture, "Seed-time," dated 1854, shows the land being ploughed with a swing plough—then rolled, and a man behind sowing broadcast.

There is an interesting note on the journey to the north of England in 1832. When Cobbett was at Hexham he remarked that " there appears to be no such thing as barns, but merely a place to take in a stack at a time, and thrash it out by a machine." Unfortunately Cobbett does not describe the machine, but we shall be doing so a little later.

In the Woodforde Diary we can watch the prices rising during the War. In Cobbett, after it, we hear of disastrous falls. At Chertsey, Surrey, in 1822, prices were less than a third of those of 1813—cows fetched £3 as against £15. Again in 1826 Cobbett went to the great fairs at Weyhill and Appleshaw, where horses, cheese, hops, corn, and 200,000 sheep were offered for sale. Ewes sold there in 1812 for 55s. to 72s., but in 1826 for only 25s. Cobbett remarks, more than once, on the great use of these markets to the small local craftsman in the old days, who, having made things, could offer them in the market directly to the purchaser.

Cobbett gives details of the labourers' wages—how in 1822 they were reduced to 6s. a week, and he met a farmer who said they must all be ruined unless they could have another " good war." Cobbett points out that Arthur Young, in 1771, allowed for a labourer, his wife, and three children, a sum which would have been equal to 13s. 1d. in 1826, instead of which he only got 8s.

There were perambulating labourers. The mowers, who were English, moved ahead of the Irish haymakers. One of their grievances was that they had to pay 5d. a quart for their beer.

Cobbett seems to have worked hard to help matters, and brought out his book on Cottage Economy—this, he claims, introduced the art of straw-plaiting into England. Certainly, until a few years ago, the cottagers in our part of the country used to plait straw, and sell it to the Luton hat manufacturers. Cobbett notes in 1826 that gloves were manufactured at Worcester which " cannot be carried on by fire or by wind or by water, and which is, therefore, carried on by the hands of human beings." The work was done by the people in their cottages and helped them very much.

Cobbett was pleasantly surprised to see a woman, near Westborough Green, in Sussex, " bleaching her home-spun and home-woven linen." He realized that if the country-side is to be healthy, farming must have its attendant trades, because they help to build up a healthy corporate life. To grow foodstuffs only, and import all your implements from factories in the towns, means a lop-sided life in both country and town.

On the other hand, at Witney, the blankets used to be made of yarn spun in the Cotswold villages, but Cobbett found that factories had been started and five of these did what thirty smaller people had done before.

Again, when Cobbett was a youth there was a cottage industry of carding and spinning wool in the Avon Valley, but this had gone when he went there on his rides. The factories in his time were not all worked by steam—he tells of woollen cloth mills all down the valley at Avening, Glos —some worked by steam, but others by water.

Still, people were trying to improve the condition of the labourer. Cobbett found allotments at Tutbury, Glos, let by a farmer to his labourers at £1 per annum per rood or ¼ acre, and he thought this was a fair rent, and that it would help the labourers, as we know it has. It was really a revival of the Common Fields, and gave men the chance to dig in the earth.

All the old crafts did not die at once. The village smith was a good tradesmen, and in between shoeing horses helped the farmers to mend the machinery which they had began to use, when it broke down. The country builder drove a good trade, as he still does to-day, but he had to be a good all-round tradesman, and be prepared to build you a house, or make you a coffin if necessary. The village wheelwright was a great artist, there is no other word, because he built the waggons. If any of our readers want to know the mysteries of this craft they have only to read "The Wheelwright Shop" by Sturt. In Fig. 95 we have illustrated various types of waggons (spelled with two g's, please) and we shall deal with this later.

It was in 1822 that Cobbett thundered against the New Turnpike Act, which sought to fit very wide wheels to the waggons, so that the tyres could be used to roll down the surface of the roads. It was an ingenious idea of the townsmen, but quite hopeless, because the moment the waggon went off the hard road on to the farm track it foundered. The Act also made chalk and lime subject to turnpike duty, and this hit the farmers of clay lands who needed lime to dress it.

One effect of the hard times was that emigration was stimulated. Cobbett remarks, in 1830, that it was " not the aged, the halt, the ailing," that were going, but the " sensible fellows " with a little money, " carpenters, wheelwrights, millwrights, smiths and bricklayers." Four hundred went from Norfolk when he was there, and they were, of course, worth their weight in gold to America. From Sheffield and district we sent knives, forks, scythes and sickles to America, but our export trade was beginning to be hampered by the tariff, passed by the U.S.A. in 1816, charging a duty on imports.

In the last paragraph is all the history of agriculture in the nineteenth century. The " sensible fellows " emigrated, and our export trade improved. The country was sacrificed to the town—the Wen had to be fed. The sickles which were exported were paid for by food for the operatives, and agriculture was left to itself, unless there happened to be a war on. The countryside became a forlorn ruin; weeds grew where once corn rustled in the wind; there were derelict farms with grass growing in their yards: we imported food, yet paid men and kept them in unemployment. The grown-ups tolerated a madder world than any a boy or girl could imagine.

Cobbett remarks on the truck or tommy system in 1830. This prevailed in the iron country of which Wolverhampton was a central point. He thought the term arose from the army, where the bread was called tommy. What the system amounted to was that the employers paid their men in commodities instead of money, and as they calculated the wages in terms of the retail prices of the goods, and bought them wholesale, they got the shop-keeper's profit for themselves. The truck system was prohibited by the Truck Act of 1831.

Cobbett found that when he went to the north in 1832 the Durham miners lived well. Their wages were 24s. a week, with house, fuel and doctoring free. As Cobbett said, " Theirs is not a life of ease to be sure, but it is not a life of hunger." They were very much better off than the unfortunate agricultural labourer.

Unfortunately Cobbett was not interested in mechanical matters. In 1830 he found that boats went up the Humber and the Ouse, to within a few miles of Leeds. He went back to Barton " by the steamboat," that is all—we should have liked a page of description. Again at North Shields, in 1832, where he found that the working people seemed to be very well off, their dwellings solid and clean, and their furniture good, he notes as well that " they have begun to make a rail-way from Carlisle to Newcastle ; and I saw them at work at it as I came along "—and no more than that of the " rail-way."

That is all we need say of Cobbett, but we strongly recommend our readers to read his " Rural Rides "— it gives one side of the picture which cannot be neglected. As well there is the man and his life. The early days at Farnham ; the father teaching his boys in the evenings ; the son's travels, and adventures, and his great courage. Turn back to our description of Newgate, and think of two years there with felons, and

L

remember that Cobbett came out unbroken. It is a splendid record.

Having gained some impressions of the life of the countryside in the early nineteenth century from Cobbett, we can now turn to the practice of agriculture, and give some details of the implements and machinery with which it was carried on. In the two words, implements and machinery, you have nearly the whole story. At the beginning of the century nearly all the implements were home-made, by local workmen, but as time went on these were replaced by machinery made in factories in the towns, and imported into the countryside, so that life there became duller as it became less varied.

If we start with the oldest of all the implements, the plough, this at an early date attracted the attention of the industrialists. Woodforde notes in his Diary, how, in 1786, he went over Mr. Ransom's new iron foundry at Norwich, and that it was " very curious indeed." Ransom introduced the chilled plough share, and by about 1825 the complete iron plough had made its appearance.

Still the townspeople did not have it all their own way, and the wooden plough held its own on heavy land; Fig. 11 was still in use when we drew it in 1919. This was more than could be said of the delightful plough we have shown in Fig. 85. We discovered this, in bits, in an orchard of a farm at Hemsby, while we were on holiday in Norfolk, and with the assistance of an old ploughman propped it up once more into a semblance of life so that we could draw it. The village laughed at the mad artist, but the old ploughman was rather touched. He held the one handle while he talked to us of his craft, and would have agreed with A. G. Street's panegyric of ploughing in " Farmers' Glory." He told us as well that he thought the plough dated from about 1840, and that it was called a Skyles plough, because it had been made by three brothers of that name who worked close by. They had their own smithy, foundry and wood-working shop

Fig. 86.—Bell's Reaping Machine (1826), now in the Science Museum, London.

Now look at Fig. 85, and decide for yourselves if they were three fools or three wise men. So far as we are concerned, we think they were artists, and we dedicate Fig. 85 to their memory, and we hope that if they are now ploughmakers in the Elysian Fields they may come to know this and give us an amused chuckle.

Following the ploughing came cultivating, harrowing and rolling, to prepare the land for sowing. It is obvious that you could not sow seed in clods.

Many more drills followed Tull's, which we illustrated in Chapter I, but, as we have seen from Cobbett, seed was still sown as well either broadcast or dibbled.

When we come to reaping, the inventors got to work at an early date, and a very natural thing happened. Their first idea was that you could not possibly take the reaping machine into a lovely field of corn, with the horse in front, and let the corn be trampled down before it could be cut, so the machine came first, and was pushed by the horses like a mowing machine. You can see at the Science Museum, London, one of the first of these reaping machines, made in 1826 by the Rev. Patrick Bell of Forfarshire, which we have shown in Fig. 86. How the unfortunate horses managed to push the cumbersome machine along over ridge and furrow we cannot imagine, but they did, and many were made and used.

Fig. 87 explains the mechanism of Bell's reaper, and it is worth consideration because it incorporated some very good ideas. The man in Fig. 86 walking on the near side of the machine was able, by means of a handle, to disconnect C from B in Fig. 87, and so stop the whole working. In the same way, by means of the cord shown, he could raise or lower the revolving frame in front to suit the height of the corn which it pressed down on to the knives. Perhaps the most ingenious idea was the pair of bevel gears at L, Fig. 87. Either of these could be slid on to M, to turn the circular shafts at the side of the sloping apron in front, on to which the corn fell when it was cut—the shafts

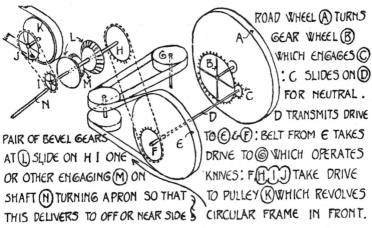

ROAD WHEEL Ⓐ TURNS
GEAR WHEEL Ⓑ
WHICH ENGAGES Ⓒ
: C SLIDES ON Ⓓ
FOR NEUTRAL.
D TRANSMITS DRIVE
TO Ⓔ & Ⓕ : BELT FROM Ε TAKES
DRIVE TO Ⓖ WHICH OPERATES
KNIVES : F Ⓗ Ⓘ TAKE DRIVE
TO PULLEY Ⓚ WHICH REVOLVES
CIRCULAR FRAME IN FRONT.

PAIR OF BEVEL GEARS
AT Ⓛ SLIDE ON H I ONE
OR OTHER ENGAGING Ⓜ ON
SHAFT Ⓝ TURNING APRON SO THAT
THIS DELIVERS TO OFF OR NEAR SIDE

FIG. 87.—The Mechanical Part of Bell's Reaping Machine.

were connected at the foot by a chain, and travelling bands
on the apron threw the corn to the near or off side as
desired. This was a real triumph. The Rev. Patrick
must have been cheered when he thought of this. His
machine could go up and down a field, and not round and
round, if so desired.

James Smith of Deanston had experimented (before
Bell) with the machine before horse type of reaper,
which rotated a cheese shaped cutter with a knife on its
lower edge.

The first real advance was made by Cyrus H. McCormick,
who patented his reaper, as Fig. 88, in U.S.A. in 1834.
McCormick's brain-wave came in realizing that if he could
only arrange his cutting knives on one side of the horse,
then the machine could be *drawn* with greater comfort.
The mechanism is shown in Fig. 88, and it is simplicity
itself, as all real brain-waves are. A pulley at the side of
the one road driving wheel was connected by a band to
another pulley over turning the circular wooden frame.
The blades of this were slightly twisted so that the corn
was gradually bent down. The bevelled gears turned a
small cranked shaft, which gave the reciprocating motion
to the cutting knife, working it backwards and forwards

127

FIG. 88.—McCormick's first Reaping Machine (1834).

like a hair clipper. McCormick's machine was a reaper only, and not a binder, and the cut corn had to be raked off and then tied up into sheaves, and stacked in stooks. The man with the rake had a tiring job, as he had to sidle along backwards, or tread on the corn as he raked it off. To get over this trouble a seat was built upon the machine, so that the raker could sit at his work—this was done in 1847, and a reaper of this type won a prize at the London Exhibition of 1851. With the McCormick reaper a pathway had to be cut all round the field first, with a scythe, to make a passage for the machine, and then round and round a diminishing square it went, driving the rabbits into an always smaller space, until they had to bolt and run the gauntlet of all the boys and dogs in the neighbourhood.

We once saw, and it is proof of our nearly incredible antiquity, a field of wheat all cut by scythe. The head man started off on the left, and cut a swathe straight ahead of him, progressing with long rhythmical strokes. When he was safely in advance, the next followed, and so on until six were stretched across in a slowly moving echelon, to the accompaniment of the most beautiful sound of the tubular straws being cut by the sharp steel. A scene as idyllic as that pictured by Hephaistos on the shield he wrought for Achilles, where the corn was cut by sickles, and the sheaf binders followed with twisted bands of straw, meanwhile a feast was made ready beneath an oak. Our reapers needed lashings of beer, and hunks of bread and cheese, with perhaps a little cold bacon, and a raw onion as savoury.

The next step to be considered is threshing. In Vol. II we illustrated the barns in which the harvest was garnered, and the flails which were used to thresh out the corn from the ear. Quite early in the eighteenth century the inventors got to work and tried to produce mechanical threshers, and by the early nineteenth century these were coming into general use. Judging by a model at the Science Museum, which we have drawn in Fig. 89, and

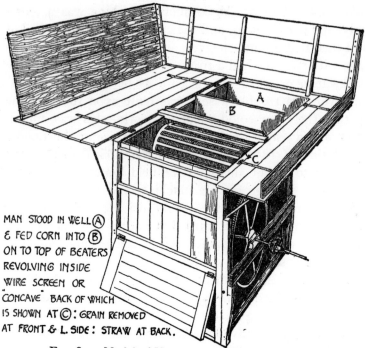

MAN STOOD IN WELL Ⓐ
& FED CORN INTO Ⓑ
ON TO TOP OF BEATERS
REVOLVING INSIDE
WIRE SCREEN OR
"CONCAVE" BACK OF WHICH
IS SHOWN AT Ⓒ: GRAIN REMOVED
AT FRONT & L. SIDE: STRAW AT BACK.

FIG. 89.—Model of Horse-power Thresher (1851).
(*Science Museum, London.*)

which was exhibited at the 1851 Exhibition, the inventors
had not made any very great progress by then, and the
early threshers were the simplest contrivances.

With the flail the corn was laid out on the threshing
floor, and the grain knocked out of the ears by the blows
of the swingel. In the early threshers the rapidly
revolving blades of the beater, shown in Fig. 90, took the
place of the swingel, and the real advance came with the
provision of the circular screen, or " concave," which
acted as a sieve and separated the grain from the straw.
This machine was worked by horse power, and its capacity
is stated to have been 60 bushels per hour. It must be
remembered that it only did the threshing, and this sifting
of the grain from the straw—it did not, as modern threshers
do, include the winnowing.

To understand winnowing, we need to go back a little.

In our book on Ancient Greece we described how the Greeks, after oxen had trodden out the corn, threw the chaff and grain up, so that the wind carried the lighter chaff away and left the heavier grain in a long shaped heap. This operation continued down through all the hundreds of years, excepting that the place of the wind was taken by the primitive fan we have illustrated in Fig. 91. One amusing detail

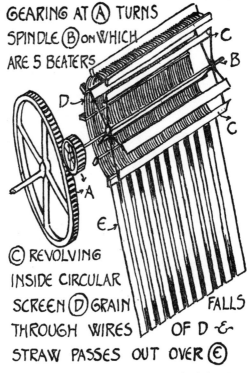

GEARING AT Ⓐ TURNS SPINDLE Ⓑ ON WHICH ARE 5 BEATERS. Ⓒ REVOLVING INSIDE CIRCULAR SCREEN Ⓓ GRAIN THROUGH WIRES STRAW PASSES OUT OVER Ⓔ ...FALLS OF D &

FIG. 90.—The Mechanical Principle of Thresher, Fig. 89.

of this method is that in throwing the grain along in front of the draught made by the fan the heaviest and best grains went farther than the poor ones, and so these, being at the tail, were called "tailings," as they still are.

One could not expect the nineteenth-century inventors to put up for long with such a simple apparatus as Fig. 91, and they very speedily invented a series of winnowing and sifting machines which got rid of the chaff, dust and weed seeds. Up till the 1851 Exhibition these had not been combined with the thresher, as they are now.

When we come to milling we have seen on p. 81 that the steam engine was applied at a very early date to mills, as was the use of cast-iron rollers, instead of the old mill

FIG. 91.—Winnowing Fan.
(*Science Museum, London.*)

stones of the windmills.   Some of the windmills continued
to hold their own, as a few of them do even to-day.

When Cobbett was at Ipswich he counted seventeen
windmills on the hills around the town, and their bodies
were painted white and their sails black.

If any of our readers wish to keep their French from
getting rusty, they can read " Lettres de Mon Moulin,"
by Alphonse Daudet.   Perhaps the nicest of the letters,
dated from an old windmill overlooking the village of
Fontvielle, in Provence, by the author of " Tartarin de
Tarascon," and which was published in a Paris newspaper,
is the one called " Le Secret de Maître Cornille."   The tale
deals with the losing fight of the old miller against the new
steam-mill.   He implores his neighbours, " N'allez pas
là-bas, disait-il ; ces brigands-là, pour faire le pain, se
servent de la vapeur, qui est une invention du diable, tandis
que moi je travaille avec le mistral et la tramontane, qui
sont la respiration du bon Dieu . . . "—but read for yourselves and find out his secret.

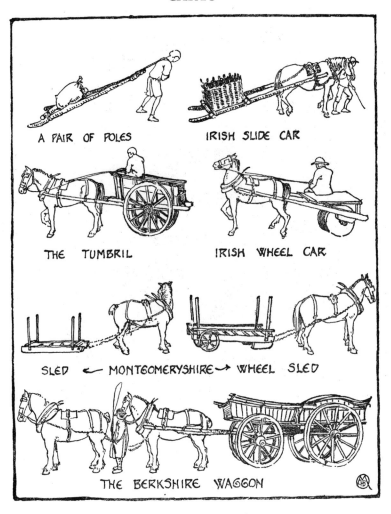

A PAIR OF POLES — IRISH SLIDE CAR

THE TUMBRIL — IRISH WHEEL CAR

SLED ← MONTGOMERYSHIRE → WHEEL SLED

THE BERKSHIRE WAGGON

FIG. 92.—Evolution of the Tumbril and Waggon.

We have illustrated the various types of windmills in Vols. I and II. Steam roller mills will hardly lend themselves to illustrations, but models can be seen at the Science Museum, London. We strongly recommend our readers who are interested to go there and see the Agricultural Section. It is the best one we know, and the Handbook on Agricultural Implements and Machinery,

FIG. 93.—An East Anglian Tumbril.
(Drawn near Halstead, Essex.)

which can be bought there for 2s., mentions, and illustrates, many other types and variations for which we cannot find space.

Now we can consider the farmer's means of transport; the tumbril that took the dung to the fields, and the waggon which carried the harvest home. Here is a subject which is nearly as old as man himself. Long before he was a farmer, he may have tied two poles together, as Fig. 92, and found that he could pull a more cumbersome load in this way than he could carry on his shoulders. When he had domesticated the horse, he could be put into the shafts, and you get the slide-car of Antrim, Ireland;

and wheels added made the Irish wheel car. Obviously this is the line of ancestry of the tumbril, or dung cart, as Fig. 93. Arranged to tip up as shown, it is one of the most useful implements on the farm. We discovered the example we have drawn near Halstead, in Essex, and as it had wooden axles (to-day these are made of hardened iron, bedded and bolted into the wooden axle-bed) it must be of very considerable age. Its wheels were 4 feet, 10 inches diameter—from the pummel or bumpers at the back to the front of the shafts was 13 feet 7 inches—the bottom frame-work was 3 feet 10 inches across the front, and 4 feet at the back, which helped the clearance of the load as it was shot out. The design of a tumbril was a nice exercise in the art of balance. If the weight is thrown too far forward on the ridge tie, or chain over the horse, it is as bad as if it is too far back, so that it pulls up on the wantie or belly-band. The old wheelwrights had to bear all these details in mind.

The waggon is nearly as old as the land over which it trundles. One of the earliest examples must be the one which was discovered in the Viking Ship at Oseberg; but with it was buried a sledge, and this seems to have been the ancestor of the waggon. A northern people would soon have discovered that the sledge slid over the snow better than dragging poles, and then, in the summer, wheels would have made the sledge go better still. Readers who are interested in the subject are advised to read Sir Cyril Fox's article in " Antiquity," which we note in our Authorities.

Here in England for centuries the waggon took the corn to market, and gaily painted (red lead for the wheels, and yellow or prussian blue for the body), with its fine team of horses, showed what manner of man the farmer was, and if he wanted to move house then the waggon was the moving van. And the last journey of all was taken in it— washed, and dressed with evergreens, the waggon carried the farmer in his coffin to the churchyard. In more ways

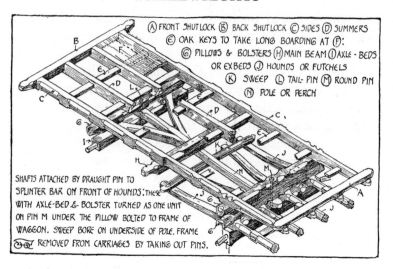

(A) FRONT SHUTLOCK (B) BACK SHUTLOCK (C) SIDES (D) SUMMERS
(E) OAK KEYS TO TAKE LONG BOARDING AT (F):
(G) PILLOWS & BOLSTERS (H) MAIN BEAM (I) AXLE - BEDS
OR EX BEDS (J) HOUNDS OR FUTCHELS
(K) SWEEP (L) TAIL- PIN (M) ROUND PIN
(N) POLE OR PERCH

SHAFTS ATTACHED BY DRAUGHT PIN TO
SPLINTER BAR ON FRONT OF HOUNDS: THESE
WITH AXLE-BED & BOLSTER TURNED AS ONE UNIT
ON PIN M UNDER THE PILLOW BOLTED TO FRAME OF
WAGGON. SWEEP BORE ON UNDERSIDE OF POLE. FRAME
REMOVED FROM CARRIAGES BY TAKING OUT PINS.

Fig. 94.—The Under-Framing and Carriages of A, Fig. 95.

than one the waggon was a very moving thing, and has
played its part well in Anglo-Saxon history. It went to
America with the emigrants, and under the " covered
waggon " the hardy frontiersman slung his plough—one
covered the ground, the other broke it.

We referred in Vol. II to " The Wheelwright's Shop,"
and should like to do so again, because in this book is given
the whole art and mystery of the wheelwright's trade as
it used to be carried on. The wheelwright was the master
craftsman of the countryside, the coach-builders generally
working in the towns. Consider the difficulty of making
a wheel by hand. To start with the face of the wheel
had to be concave or dished in design. This was done
because when the waggon went bumping over the ridges
the whole weight of its load might be delivered as a thrust
on the inside of the stock (nave or hub). Had the wheel
been made flat, the weight of such a blow would have
knocked all the spokes out, so the wheel was dished.
Consider the difficulties this entailed. The stocks were of
elm, and in the early days chipped out by hand with an
axe, because they had not got lathes to do it. The spokes,

WAGGON AT TRING HERTS. DRAWN 1919
BODY 12'·0" LONG ~ FRONT WHEELS 3'·9"DIAM.
BACK WHEELS 4'·9" DIAM.

A

B

WAGGON AT HALSTEAD ESSEX (1932)
BODY 11'·9" FRONT WHEELS 3'·11"DIAM. BACK 5'·1".

C

WAGGON AT
TRING (1920)
BODY 12'×3'·9"
FRONT WHEELS 4'·0" DIAM.
BACK WHEELS 4'·11"DIAM.

C.H.B.Q.

FIG. 95.—Various Types of Waggons.

made of heart of oak, and cleft, not sawn, were tenoned into the stock in a staggered fashion, one forward, one back, so as not to weaken the stock, and as the spokes not only radiated but leaned out a little, cutting the mortises called for judgment. Then there was the further complication of the felloes, or rims, of ash, elm or beech; these were made in sections and dowelled together and had to be mortised to take the spokes, which were always arranged in pairs, but owing to the dishing of the wheels the spoke at the bottom was vertical, and the one over leaned out, and the felloes had to be fitted together to make a rim and yet pick up all the spoke tenons. Then the tyres, which by reason of the dishing of the wheels were not like narrow widths of a cylinder, but had to be slightly conoid in shape.

Another refinement of waggon building was the fitting of lengthways floorboards, as Fig. 94. The floor of a waggon is supported by the " sides " outside, and the " summers " inside, which act as joists. As these run longitudinally the simplest method of flooring would have been to nail the floorboards across these, but it would not have been so good, because shovelling out a load across the grain of the floorboards would have worn and splintered them. So oak keys were driven through the summers from side to side and kept down about 1 inch below them, and the floorboards fitted between lengthways. Mr. Sturt says in his book that in Surrey this thoroughly practical method was given up about 1884 for the cheaper, and nastier, cross-flooring.

All these details and many things beside are discussed in Sturt's book, and when reading this look at Will Hammond's and George Cook's photographs, and think of them as great artists, because that is what they were. They and their master were playing a losing game, which they have now lost, and passed on—the machine was too much for them—and in losing them we have lost something as well. Men who with oak, ash and elm, a few tools and

C.H.B.Q.

BERKSHIRE WAGGON (DRAWN 1933) BODY 12'6" LONG: FRONT WHEELS 4'6" DIAM. BACK WHEELS 5'5": TRACK OVERALL 5'7": VERMILION WHEELS: YELLOW BODY.

Fig. 96.—A Waggon from the Vale of the White Horse.

that most wonderful tool of all, the human hand, could make a waggon are a loss. It is saddening to think that you would hardly find a man in England to-day, unless you happened on a very old man, who could do their work. There are many though who, if asked to do so with such a simple apparatus, would sit down and weep. When a waggon was finished in Sturt's shop the fact was celebrated by a wayzgoose, or supper, held in the local inn, with songs and merriment.

Fig. 95 shows various types of waggons which we have drawn from time to time. A, though not of very interesting shape, was one of the most beautifully made waggons we have ever come across, and the waggon chamfering, which had the practical purpose of reducing weight, was superb. For example, look at the strouters or struts on the sides. Its under-framing is shown in Fig. 94. B, Fig. 95, might be nearly as interesting in shape as the old Berkshire waggon, Fig. 96, because it is of the waisted variety, but the waist is concealed by the sides being taken across it, with a hole cut in to take the wheel on the lock. The front ladder and movable front are unusual. It was said to be about sixty years old. C, Fig. 95, is a Wiltshire type which had found its way to Tring.

A and C, Fig. 95, were broken up for scrap-iron and firewood soon after we drew them.

Some of these drawings date from 1919–20, when we were engaged in a campaign to try and get some specimens saved, with other implements, in an open-air museum. Our campaign naturally did not come to anything—people are not really interested—but here is a letter, dated April 7th, 1921, from Thomas Hardy, who was an architect before he became a novelist and poet, and whose help we had solicited:

" The commendable interest you take, as is shown by the letter you send me, in old agricultural implements as valuable relics of the past, I entirely reciprocate, and were I younger I might assist you in steps towards the preserva-

Fig. 97.—The Wheelwright's Shop at Beckley, Sussex.
After a painting by P. W. Cole, R.B.A., A.R.C.A. (Lond.).

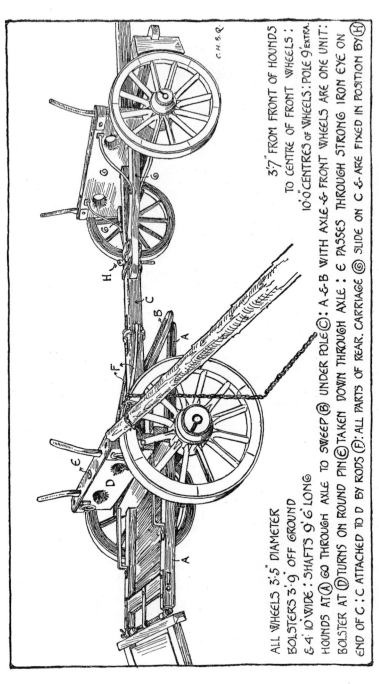

ALL WHEELS 3'·5 DIAMETER
BOLSTERS 3'·9 OFF GROUND
& 4'·10 WIDE : SHAFTS 9'·6 LONG
HOUNDS AT ⒶGO THROUGH AXLE TO SWEEP Ⓑ UNDER POLE Ⓒ: A & B WITH AXLE & FRONT WHEELS ARE ONE UNIT :
BOLSTER AT ⒹTURNS ON ROUND PIN Ⓔ TAKEN DOWN THROUGH AXLE : E PASSES THROUGH STRONG IRON EYE ON
END OF C : C ATTACHED TO D BY RODS Ⓕ: ALL PARTS OF REAR CARRIAGE Ⓖ SLIDE ON C & ARE FIXED IN POSITION BY Ⓗ

3'·7 FROM FRONT OF HOUNDS
TO CENTRE OF FRONT WHEELS :
10'·0 CENTRES OF WHEELS : POLE 9' EXTRA.

C. H. B. Q.

FIG. 98.—The Timber Carriage. (Drawn at Potten End, Herts, 1933.)

SHAFTS
7'3" TO 1ST BAR PLUS
10FT TO CENTRE OF 6FT DIAM.
WHEELS: JIB 10FT LONG:
LOG RAISED BY INNER CHAIN ON JIB
WOUND UP BY WINCH IN FRONT: ENDS
OF THIS CHAIN THROWN OVER
DRUM THUS ⬚ TAKE HELD TIGHT
BY WEIGHT: OUTER CHAIN HOOKED TO AXLE
TAKES WEIGHT IF JIB IS RELEASED TO RAISE LOG HIGHER.

Fig. 99.—The Timber Truck, Neb or Bob.   (Drawn at Berkhamsted, Herts.).

tion of typical examples. But I am quite unable for one reason and another to join actively in such a movement. Letters to the papers invariably bring an overwhelming correspondence, which I cannot cope with at my age. I trust that you will be able to enlist the sympathies of more active lovers of such antiquities before it is too late to do anything towards saving them.

" The farm waggon, of which you send a sketch [this was C, Fig. 95] is a fairly good specimen ; but the old ones left hereabout—at any rate till lately—are more graceful, the curve being very marked, and the floral designs painted on the front and tail-board very ingenious. This latter feature has, however, almost disappeared under a coat of plain paint." We have never discovered a waggon with floral designs.

This was before we had drawn the old Berkshire waggon (Fig. 96) in 1933, and we think this would have earned Hardy's commendation. We discovered it late in the autumn of 1932, when we were motoring through Tom Brown's country, the Vale of the White Horse, Berkshire. The wide wheels with the double strakes, locking felloe to felloe, were seen in the gloom of a cart-shed by the road. The ancient Cowley we possess was stopped with a shriek of its brakes, and we tip-toed into the shed and found Fig. 96. It was a wonderful moment, because—let there be no mistake about it—we were in the presence of as fine a piece of evidence of the ingenuity of man as well could be—a wooden ship and a waggon such as this are two of the most beautiful things ever made by man, and this type of waggon is so ship-like. It is of the waisted variety, as was the Kent and Sussex type we illustrated in Fig. 118, Vol. II, and the floor rises up towards the front. Now think how you would like to make this in such a workshop as Fig. 97, without anything to help you except your brain, hands and a few tools. The Berkshire waggon may still exist (we drew it in the spring of 1933), so we send out another plea. Cannot we somehow or other start an open-air

FIG. 100.—Ploughing (with a Wooden Plough), Rolling and Broadcast Sowing, c. 1850.

(Victoria and Albert Museum, London.

By J. F. Herring.

FIG. 101.—A Catholic Town in 1440.

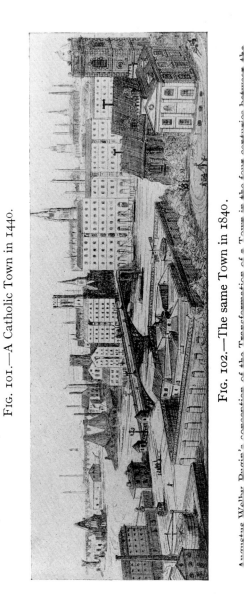

FIG. 102.—The same Town in 1840.

Augustus Welby Pugin's conception of the Transformation of a Town in the four centuries between the

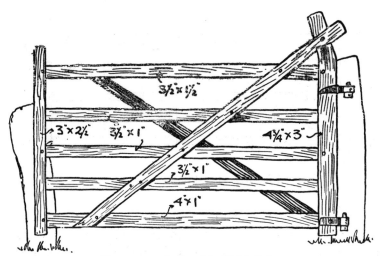

FIG. 103.—A Cornish Field-Gate.
8 feet wide by 4 feet high.

museum, like the Skansen, near Stockholm, where the
pleasant old things of the countryside could be preserved.
It is not well for us that they should all be destroyed.
The average weight of a waggon was about 18 cwt., and
it carried a 3-ton load. In 1772 Young noted the cost of
a waggon at £20 to £25, and a tumbril £10 to £12. By
1870 a waggon cost £42.

The wheelwright's work started in the woods; here
he bought his timber, and he had to buy with judgment.
Naturally curved trunks would cut into the curved timbers
which were used in waggon building, and you did not buy
your oak and elm in the same woods, because oak likes a
heavy soil, and elm grows on gravel. Having bought your
timber, you carted it home and cut it up over a pit, with
a top sawyer and a bottom sawyer, and then it was stacked
in the yard to season, at least a year for each inch in
thickness—laid down almost like port to mature, and used
with the same judgment and gratitude.

All this meant work for other people besides the wheelwright—his timber had to be carried. Fig. 98 shows the
timber carriage which was, and is still, used. In form it

145

FIG. 104—The Five-barred Gate.

much resembles the frame of the farm waggon, without the body on it—in fact, this timber carriage is really the basis on which many carriage and coach forms have been built up ; a few boards laid across it, and one edgeways up against each standard and you had a very useful waggon. The carriages could be used as well for carrying hop-poles to the hop-gardens, and for a variety of other purposes. When the carriage is used in the woods it is brought up as close to the side of the log as is possible, then larch poles are placed on wheels as shown. These are held in position by a chain taken through the pillow, under the felloe, round over the larch pole and the tyre under the felloe and then hooked as shown. The other ends of the chains are passed under the log and over it, and back over the carriage to the horses on the other side, who then pull on the chains and roll the log up the poles until it rests on the carriage, butt end always foremost. The moment the pull of the horses is put on the chain the tops of the poles are locked to the wheels by the methods of fixing the chains there ; a very simple but ingenious arrangement. The carriage is low built and wide, as it need be to prevent overturning.

But some logs are so awkwardly placed that the carriage cannot be brought alongside them, and then in our part of the country the truck, neb, or bob, as Fig. 99, is used. We cannot say anything of this amazing contrivance, or how many centuries have gone to its evolution, but here it is still in use. The truck is backed over the butt end of the log, which is raised as described on the drawing. Two horses are used on the road, driven tandem, so that the total length with log is about 37 feet, and to see a truck like this on the road alongside a Green Line bus is to see old and new together in a startling fashion. Figs. 103 and 104 show field gates; these used to be locally made and, like the waggons, the patterns varied in the different localities. A good gate is not at all an easy thing to design; you lose the simplicity which is necessary and produce something which looks as if it should be seen in front of a villa unless you are very careful.

Here we must finish our sections on the countryside and the work of the farmer, and we are conscious that we have done it badly. Still there may be something in it which will stir the imagination of the boys and girls for whom we write. Remember the rejoinder of Alexander to Dinocrates, that, " as an infant is nourished by the milk of its mother, depending thereon for its progress to maturity, so a city depends on the fertility of the country surrounding it for its riches." From the attic in which this is being written we look out on an awakening world; the blackthorn is in full flower, with the cherry and plum, and the bees are hard at work on the arabis and aubretia. The thorn has put out its leaves, but the other trees only show tender flushes of colour through which their branches can be seen. A glossy starling has perched on the bare ash opposite our window and, having parted company with the flock, has set up housekeeping with another on the chimney top—the spring is here.

This miraculous place, this English countryside, is worth knowing and preserving and loving—we commend it to English town-dwelling boys and girls. Adrian Bell's and A. G. Street's books will help us to understand it, and we must not forget " Joseph and His Brethren."

CHAPTER VII

NINETEENTH-CENTURY BUILDING

W HEN we come to building at the beginning of the
nineteenth century we find a very different state
of affairs from that which had obtained at the beginning
of the eighteenth. When Queen Anne was on the throne
there was one central stream still steadily flowing from its
sources in Jones and Wren. One hundred years on, the
stream had divided up into many rivulets and had lost
its force and direction. It was possible in building to be
Greek or Goth, Roman, Chinese or Egyptian—fashion
had taken the place of tradition.

We will deal with the "Goths" first, because in the end
they triumphed over the "Greeks" and sacked their citadels.

We have seen (p. 48) how early the first Gothic
revival started; Battey Langley published his book in
1742, and in it set out to restore and improve Gothic
architecture. Horace Walpole was certainly no fool, and
yet he attempted the impossible in building a castle.

In the second Gothic revival of the nineteenth century
the full tide of romanticism set in, and flowered into the
poetry of Sir Walter Scott, which preceded the beginning
of the Waverley Novels in 1814. The ferment in men's
minds which produced the French Revolution was reflected
in their buildings—the rules of Classical Architecture were
thrown on one side for what was thought to be the more
natural inspiration of Gothic. Picturesqueness was demanded, so castles and abbeys were explored. Their lovely
ruins, seen perhaps by night, with a pale moon silvered
against the gloom, and showing through the web of a rose
window, fired the clients and their architects. So they set
out to recreate castles and abbeys, forgetting entirely that
you cannot *design* castles and abbeys, but that these must
grow out of quite definite practical requirements and plans.

In our book on Anglo-Saxon England we showed how

FIG. 105.—Midday Traffic in Parliament Street (1829).

By E. Lami & H. Monnier.

Fig. 106.—Interior of the ' Reduced Annuities,' Bank of England.

the timber forts on the tops of the mounts, as shown in the
Bayeux Tapestry, developed into the Shell Keep, as at
Berkhampstead. In Vol. I. of this series the square keep
of Hedingham was followed by the polygonal one at
Orford, in Suffolk, and then the fortified walls of the
Edwardian castles in Wales gradually developed into the
more comfortable quarters at Bodiam. Again, in Vol. I.
we showed how the conventual buildings of the Bene-
dictines, Cistercians or Carthusians developed around their
cloistered needs. The original builders of both castles and
abbeys put plan and practical purposes first, and built
around these beautifully ; they did not set out to construct picturesqueness ; they ornamented construction
instead of constructing ornament ; the nineteenth-century
Gothicists did not follow their good example. Take
Ashridge, Herts, the subject of our sketches Figs. 107 and
108. This was designed by James Wyatt (1746–1813), who
was afterwards called the Destroyer by Augustus Welby
Pugin. This was because of the work Wyatt did when
" restoring " Salisbury Cathedral in 1789, when he took
out thirteenth-century glass like that of the Five Sisters
at York. This was hardly a good preparation for the work
carried out at Ashridge from 1806–13, and which was
finished by Wyatt's nephew. We have chosen Ashridge
because we used to go there in the old days when it was
still a house, and not a college as it is now. Look at the
exterior view, Fig. 107, and it is just a muddle. Had it
been a real castle, abbey or house you would have been
able to pick out its plan or skeleton at once. There is no
recognizable make or shape about Ashridge. It is like a
snowman, built up by sticking on lumps instead of having
good bones inside it. Internally it was much the same ;
you entered, by the door shown in the distance in Fig. 108,
into an entrance hall with a timbered roof, which was much
too high for its length and width, and looked through a
double-arcaded screen, carrying the bedroom passages, into
the staircase hall shown in our sketch. All this magnificence

Fig. 107.—Ashridge Park, Hertfordshire.

(*James Wyatt, Architect. 1806–13.*)

led up to a smallish ante-room, with the dining-room on one side and the state drawing-rooms on the other. The staircase hall, about 40 feet square, rises up some 90 feet odd, so that it is a " Gothick " well, made up of bits, and without any pride of race or ancestry behind it. No real Gothic staircase was ever like this one.

Here is a tale which illustrates the early nineteenth-century outlook, and how cheerfully they destroyed to make way for their own work. We were shown a nice eighteenth-century barometer in a mahogany wall case and told that this was all that remained of the furniture of the house which preceded Ashridge. When the new house was ready all the old furniture was piled up in the park and a lovely bonfire made of it, and all the village watched the conflagration, including the parson of Little Gaddesden, and then suddenly the weather glass, untouched by the flames, slithered down off the pile to his feet, and he whipped it up and put it under his cloak, and many years later it came back to Ashridge and was treasured as an " antique."

Wyatt was the architect of the sham abbey which Beckford built at Fonthill in 1795, which fell down soon after.

The next names in importance in the Gothic revival were the Pugins, father and son. The elder Pugin came to London in 1798, and was employed by Nash. He had a drawing school and published " Specimens of Gothic Architecture, 1821-3." His son, Augustus Welby Northmore Pugin (1812-52), followed in his father's footsteps, and as a boy of fourteen was measuring up Rochester Castle and nearly lost his life by the collapse of trenches which he had excavated. Augustus Welby became a Roman Catholic in 1834, and one of his works which Londoners can study is the Roman Catholic cathedral in Southwark. He also assisted Barry with the designs of the Houses of Parliament, in Westminster, begun in 1840, and clothed the classic type of plan with the Gothic detail one sees there now.

Pugin published his " Contrasts," or a parallel between the architecture of the fifteenth and nineteenth centuries, in 1836. Figs. 101 and 102, reproduced from one of the original plates, shows one of the contrasts. One of his last works (before he died in 1852) was the arrangement of the Mediæval Court of the Great Exhibition of 1851. In an illustrated " cyclopædia " published in 1852 one of the exhibits in the Mediæval Court, an oak niche, is noted as " the great peculiarity of this niche consists in its being designed after the old principle, to suit the material in which it has been executed." This was more than could be said of many of the exhibits. Fig. 126 shows a table designed by the Duchess of Sutherland, and made for her by G. J. Morant. It is described as being of elegant design and the finest workmanship. The swans were painted white, and the lilies and bulrushes partly gilt and partly white. We hope her Grace was a better duchess than designer.

Pugin was the pioneer of the later Gothic revival, which came about as a response to the movement which originated at Oxford when Keble preached a sermon on National Apostacy on July 14th, 1833. Under Keble and Pusey the movement quickened the life of the English Church. Henceforward Greek churches, like Inwood's at St. Pancras, were thought of as pagan and became unfashionable, and the many new churches which were built in the middle and later part of the nineteenth century had to be Gothic, and they were not very much nearer the truth than Ashridge, which we have illustrated. The best summing up of the later Gothic revival we know was contained in a letter written to us by the late R. Norman Shaw, R.A., in 1910 : " It was always supposed that ' Gothic ' was to develop, and there was any amount of tall talk as to what it was to do—but it didn't do anything. It was like a cut flower—pretty enough to look at—but fading away before your eyes—and if we don't take care, the English Renaissance that we now have will do the same—so unlike the French—they went on all the last century doing work

FIG. 108.—Ashridge Park, Hertfordshire.
Staircase Hall.

(*James Wyatt, Architect*, 1806–13.

that was founded on their old work, and magnificent work it was—and this was the result of gentle development, new features and arrangements growing from the old stock. In fact their Architecture was alive—ours dead—a mighty difference—and arising of course from their having a School—and we have none." Norman Shaw was old in 1910, and had retired after a distinguished career as an architect in the nineteenth century. Some representative examples of houses designed by him are shown in Volume IV of "Everyday Things". We remember that it was a little saddening at the time to receive the letter and realize how the high hopes had faded. The "castle," "abbey," "cathedral" and "church" builders had discovered that architecture is not a "cut flower" which can be used for decorative purposes and put in any pot—but a plant that only flowers if it is rooted in reality.

Still the Gothic people did not have it all their own way, and the old classical tradition lingered on side by side with the Gothic until well on in the nineteenth century. The Prince of Wales became Regent in 1811, and George III. did not die until 1820. It was during the Regency that Regent Street, London, was designed by John Nash, and a very noble piece of town planning it was. Starting at Regent's Park with the villas there, it finished at Carlton House, where the Regent lived, and where Carlton House Terrace and the Duke of York's column were built when Carlton House itself was pulled down (1827–29). The Regent's Park villas remain, but Regent Street has gone, and in 1933 a beginning was made in the destruction of Carlton House Terrace, which it is hoped will not continue. Nash's architecture was not in itself superb—there is the well-known quip,

"But is not our Nash, too, a very great master ;
He finds us all brick and he leaves us all plaster,"—

it was the fact that Regent Street was part of a well-ordered scheme which made it such a distinguished and well-mannered street. Now all the buildings are up and down—there is no plan—and the street is just a medley of

FIG. 109.—View of Brighton looking to Holland's Pavilion before it was orientalised by Nash, 1839.

By John Bruce, Brighton.

FIG. 110.—Wedgwood and Byerley's Pottery Emporium, York Street, St. James's Square, *c.* 1809.

FIG. 111.—A fine Shop in Artillery Row, Houndsditch, London, of the latter half of the eighteenth century.

Fig. 112.—House at Kennington Oval, South London.   (Now demolished.)

poor architectural forms. The old Regent Street was better than the new, and here we should like to tell of the Bath buns bought there when we were young. The ones we used to eat there seemed incomparably better than their unworthy successors; it is sad to think we shall never again feast our eyes on their yellow sweetness, never surreptitiously lick our fingers after the eating!

But to revert to architecture. During this time many houses were built; the Napoleonic wars were at an end and much building was done. The plastered houses were made gay with paint and balconies were added in delicate Greek designs. In Fig. 120 we show a quiet interior in one of these nice stucco squares, and from the tailpieces (pp. 183, 197) you can see how charming were these neo-Greek interiors; they are taken from Moses' delicate little engravings called "Modern Costume," 1825. Donald Pilcher has given us an entertaining study of this time in his "Regency Style" (1948), in which the varied architectural fashions are linked up with contemporary social life.

Another name to be mentioned honourably is that of Sir John Soane. He was born in 1753, entered the office of George Dance in 1768, won the R.A. Gold Medal 1776, travelled in Italy 1778–80 and, coming home, was from 1788 architect to the Bank of England, London, for forty-five years. Soane's screen walls to the Bank building still remain, and Fig. 106 shows one of his interiors there. This is curiously modern in design—all the architectural fripperies have gone by the board; except for the little columns in the cupola light there are not any orders with their entablatures, and the effect is got by simply ornamented geometrical shapes. Soane was a very sound constructor, and his vaults were made up of fireproof tiles, not lath and plaster. His work did not please his contemporaries, who were outraged by its modernity. The house which he built for himself in Lincoln's Inn Fields, London, and which is now the Soane Museum, should be visited because the furniture is as he left it. Soane

FIG. 113.—Houses in Brunswick Square, Hove, Sussex.

installed a small pipe high-pressure steam-heating system in his own house in 1831, but had used steam heating at Tyringham, Buckinghamshire, as early as 1797. Here is an interesting point: the long hours which were worked at this time in the new factories are often noted as being inhuman, but these were not unusual. Soane's office hours were seven to seven in the summer, and eight to eight in the winter.

Fig. 112 shows one of the suburban houses which began to be built early in the nineteenth century, and what could be more pleasant than this one which used to stand at Kennington Oval? One likes to think of a nice young couple setting up house in it. We remember it when going to the Oval in the old days, but even then it had fallen on evil times and looked unkempt. When the house was built, Kennington and Camberwell were countrified to the business man, and he lived there and drove into the City. Now these neighbourhoods are forlorn wildernesses; many of the old houses remain, but they are unkempt and uncared for. On some of the front gardens cheap shops have been built; in others a few sooty shrubs remain, and gates hang awry and creak dismally.

Many very pleasant Regency houses and shops remain at Brighton—quite enough to make one sad that the town was developed so badly during the later nineteenth century. Had the Regent's tradition of building been carried on and developed it might be quite one of the pleasantest towns in England.

It is rather terrifying that from the Town Surveyor's Department has come the proposal to pull down some of the charming old Regency squares, and build enormous blocks of modern flats on their sites, an enormity which it is hoped will be defeated. (There is much more interest in Regency work, and two very charming exhibitions, sponsored by the Member of Parliament, have been held at Brighton.)

Fig. 113 shows one or two of the houses in Brunswick Square, Hove, Sussex, and here the Ionic order from the Erechtheum, Athens, which we saw in our book on

Fig. 114.—In the Park (1825). The North Lodge, Stanhope Gate, Hyde Park, London.

(*Decimus Burton, Architect, 1800—1881.*)

FIG. 115.—East Front of the Pavilion, Brighton.

Classical Greece, on one house has been pleasantly varied with plain pilasters on the next. Decimus Burton's Hyde Park lodges, as Fig. 114, carry on the Greek tradition.

Again, what could be more pleasant or conducive to good business than the old shops we illustrate in Figs. 110, 111 ? The modern multiple stores are the great offenders—they come into the country towns and buy, perhaps, a nice old Georgian house, and tear out half of its front. Then up goes an enormous name plate, and if they can contrive that this goes half across the first-floor windows, then this is done. Under and behind an enormous sheet of plate glass loads of provisions are displayed for sale as an amusement park for all the flies in the neighbourhood. They seem to advertise quantity, but not quality.

It was at Brighton that the Regent built the Pavilion, between the years of 1784 and 1820. Starting as a respectable farm-house, it was continually being altered and enlarged until it came to its present form. Holland, the architect of Carlton House in London, made it into a quite nice and ordinary house from whence the Regent could enjoy the sea breezes and lead the fashion in going to the seaside. Repton prepared designs, and published them in 1808, and these seem to have given ideas to Nash, who gave the Pavilion its present exotic form. Cobbett was in Brighton in 1822, and this is how he describes the building : " Where you see the thing from a distance, you think you see a parcel of cradle-spits [one is shown in Fig. 133] of various dimensions, sticking up out of the mouths of so many enormous squat decanters. Take a square box, the sides of which are three feet and a half, and the height a foot and a half. Take a large Norfolk turnip, cut off the green of the leaves, leave the stalks 9 inches long, tie these round with a string 3 inches from the top, and put the turnip on the middle of the top of the box. Then take four turnips of half the size, treat them in the same way, and put them on the corners of the box. Then take a considerable number of bulbs of the crown-imperial,

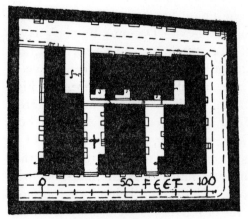

FIG. 116.—Housing in a Slum Area.

the narcissus, the hyacinth, the tulip, the crocus, and others ; let the leaves of each have sprouted to about an inch, more or less according to the size of the bulb ; put all these, pretty promiscuously, but pretty thickly, on the top of the box. Then stand off and look at your architecture. There! That's 'a Kremlin'!"

Naturally enough Cobbett thought the Pavilion was a vain thing, and, knowing as he did the unfortunate condition of the agricultural labourer at the time, he was enraged that money should have been wasted in such a way. Still from our point of view the Regent's seaside palace is very interesting, and one can hardly understand the Regency Period unless a visit is paid to Brighton to see it. On a grey day it is very unreal, but in sunlight, or at night when it is floodlit and seen by itself behind the silhouette of trees which cut off the rest of the town, the east front, as Fig. 115, becomes a fairy palace, and one sees what the old Regent was aiming at.

Inside, the State apartments are very fine with their riotous decorations (Figs. 80A, 80B) in silver, scarlet, gold and writhing dragons, all in the Chinese manner. The frontispiece shows a banquet and will give some idea of the colour.

Fig. 109, from a very interesting old print of Brighton, shows the first view of the town which the traveller from London had, with the earlier Pavilion as its central feature.

But enough of kings' palaces. The time has come to write of other things ; so far we have been concerned with beauty, now we must search for ugliness, and we shall not have to go very far. In the nineteenth century people seem

FIG. 117.—A Factoryscape in the Potteries.

Fig. 119.—One-Roomed House for Five.

Fig. 118.—Back-to-Back Houses in the North

o

FIG. 120.—A Family Party in 1806.

to have lost all their architectural good manners. Until then even the simplest buildings, the cottages, stables and sheds, were pleasantly simple and unpretentious, and you could live in and with them. There was no need to have a Society for the Preservation of Rural England. Since the Industrial Revolution the very reverse has come to be the case, and building has been unplanned and marked by pretentious shoddiness. It was not till 1909 that John Burns brought in his Town Planning Bill to try and persuade people that it was a good idea to plan a town before you built it.

Let us take Fig. 3 for an example. If you happened to find your way to Berkhampstead and wandered around the little town, as a stranger you would be able to trace its history since the day that William the Conqueror accepted the submission of the English there. The place was vulgarized in the nineteenth century; there have been hideous suburban developments, and multiple shops spoil the High Street. Still the town is a microcosm, a little world of its own, and recognizable as such.

Now let us take an Automobile Association map and select one of those areas which are hatched in grey as places to be avoided if you are motoring for pleasure. The hatching is symbolical, and the warning necessary. These industrial towns are grey beyond belief, pleasure has flown away, and you are apt to lose your way because the place has been developed without any plan—it is, in fact, without form and void. There may be a church, but there are more likely to be many chapels where people can voice their dissent. There will hardly be a market square; there is no need for one, because the products of the factories are sold overseas and paid for by imported foodstuffs. So the town has no centre, and as it has no plan you will find factories, houses, shops, chapels, cemeteries all in one inextricable jumble. Around the town will be the later suburban developments. Miles of dreary roads and houses; a growth which has spread across the fields like a fungus, but always cut off from the country by a tin-can zone where the urban rubbish is shot. If you can imagine yourself as having come from Mars with a seeing eye, and seeing for the first time, the first question which would arise would surely be : What were the conditions of life which produced so much ugliness ? If a man is to be judged by his

FIG. 121.—Early Nineteenth-Century Chair.

works, how are we to judge these early Industrialists ? They acquired money, but not much else.

If our books have served any useful purpose at all, it will be found in the fact that throughout them all we have stressed the fact that life and things must be planned ; that you cannot *design* buildings. These must grow naturally out of the practical requirements of people, and the buildings are like the people. Take any period you like and study the people and their ways, and you will find that their buildings fit them like gloves.

All the king's horses, and men, and architects, and town planners, and Acts of Parliament must fail unless the conditions of life are kindly and pleasant.

All this leads up to the slums, which remain as a source of embarrassment to the industrial towns, because, to give them what credit we can, they are doing their best to remedy matters. Fig. 118 shows a court in a slum area

o*

FIG. 122.—Early Nineteenth-Century Chair.
About 1806.

in an industrial town in the North of England, which shall be nameless, and the photograph was taken in February, 1933. It shows typical back-to-back houses, built perhaps 100 years ago. Back to back means that the houses are only one room deep, so at the back of the houses shown on each side of the court in Fig. 118 comes another house stuck on to it. Each house is about 11 feet wide, and 11 feet 6 inches from front to back. There is no back garden or yard, and the only chance of light and sun is the one window on to the court. There is only one room and the staircase on each floor, and the staircase opens into each room and is not cut off by a passage. Each room may have its family (see Fig. 119), and there are others in the cellars to which the outer stairs lead down. It is only a year or so since the Thames rose very rapidly and, overflowing the Embankment, drowned many people living in cellars at Westminster, within a few hundred yards of the Houses of Parliament.

There are no conveniences in the houses—never a larder, for example. The one water-tap is shown in the court over the pails (Fig. 118), and water has to be fetched from this for all the families, no matter what the weather is like. The doors on each side of the tap and pails are the closets, and there is none in the houses. The smaller door just to the right of the water-tap served for the removal of the sewage from the closets. The only sink is the channel in the paving of the court, and the dustbins stand there to aid the general frowstiness.

Fig. 116 shows a block plan of the area, and a cross marks the position of the court shown in Fig. 118. There are twenty-eight houses in the island, and including half the area of the surrounding streets that gives 127 houses to the acre. The new garden cities aim at not more than twelve. Here is an interesting point : we think the final solution of the slum problem will be found in crowding far more than 127 houses on to the acre, and for this reason. The slum dweller is such a long-tailed town mouse that if you take him into the country, where the mice have short tails, he is unhappy. He misses the noise and the excitement, and to walk along a country lane at night, without any lamps, reduces him to panic fear, especially if an owl screeches ; so the transported slum-dweller wants to go back to the friendly town. Then he is so poor that he cannot afford the pence for fares to reach his work. As well, garden cities are far too expensive. Spreading the houses over such a wide area of ground means costly roads, paths, sewers, gas, water and electric light mains, and every individual house has to heat its own water, cook, and so on. Instead of spoiling the country, we think it would be better to take the trees and grass into the towns. Don't rebuild the slums ; blow them up with dynamite, then build great towers of dwellings and surround them with gardens. Let the flats have hot water and heating laid on, and all the conveniences. Hitler has helped towards this in various places.

A boy or girl reading this book may become a great town-planner ; they may even build Jerusalem in England's green and pleasant land. It would be a great work.

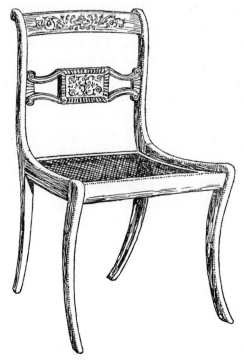

FIG. 123.—Chair, about 1820.

Though many back-to-back slum houses still remain to-day, desperate efforts are being made to clear them away. A few years ago one of the northern towns had 25,000 such houses, which was later reduced to 2,500. Unfortunately the slum represents valuable property, showing a good return on your money. So they have been acquired by people who have invested their savings in this way, or by speculators whose idea was to buy cheap and let dear, and these people represent the vested interests.

Before a slum can be cleared away the municipality has to gather all this information together and prepare a scheme for rebuilding; the Ministry of Health sends down an inspector, who holds an inquiry and hears all the evidence and objections. All this adds to cost, and sometimes the new buildings are too expensive for the old inhabitants, who just move on to another slum. It is all very difficult and complicated and hopeless; everybody wishes the slums to disappear, yet they persist.

Sir Edwin Chadwick (1800–1890) was a pioneer in the attempt to improve the conditions of the working classes. In 1832 he was appointed Assistant Commissioner for an inquiry into the working of the Poor Laws; in 1833 into

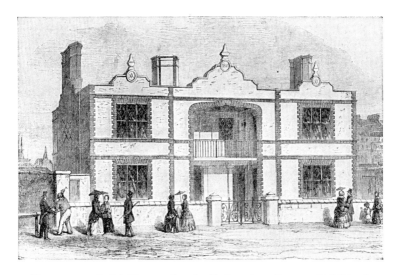

FIG. 124.—Model Houses for the Labouring Classes, Exhibited by Prince Albert at the Exhibition of 1851.

FIG. 125.—A Pair of Labourer's Cottages.
(*From " Designs for Cottages and Schools " by John Hall,* 1825)

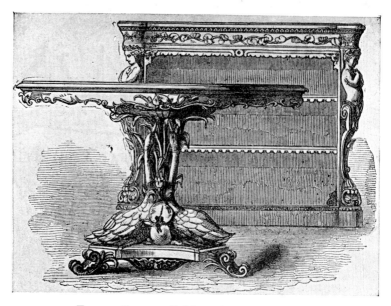

FIGS. 126, 127.—Table and Bookcase, 1851.

By G. J. Morant.

FIG. 128.—Piano in Papier-mâché Case.

FURNITURE AT THE GREAT EXHIBITION, 1851.

FIG. 129.—Brass Inlay in Rosewood on Top-rail of FIG. 123.

factory life ; in 1834 was Secretary of the Poor Law Board ; in 1838 carried out investigations into the sanitary condition of London. All this led up to his " Survey into the Sanitary Conditions of the Labouring Classes of Great Britain " and the appointment of Medical Officers of Health. While Chadwick and his colleagues were making this survey " it was frequently declared by the inmates that they had never for many years witnessed the approach or presence of persons of that condition near them," and Chadwick declared that " more filth, worse physical suffering and moral disorder than Howard describes as affecting the prisoners, are to be found among the cellar population of the working people of Liverpool, Manchester or Leeds." Again, Chadwick found that in Bath in 1837 small-pox carried off 300 slum dwellers, " but scarcely one gentleman and only two or three tradesmen."

When Chadwick died he left a large sum of money in trust for delivering lectures on the promotion of sanitary science, and these are still given.

Another pioneer in the cause was Prince Albert, the husband of Queen Victoria, and the great-grandfather of our present King. Readers of Lytton Strachey's " Queen Victoria " will remember his appreciation of the character of the Prince Consort, and the interest which he took in science and industry, and Strachey points out the great difficulties which the Prince encountered when he first suggested the idea of a Great Exhibition to be held in London in 1851 ; how these were overcome and the idea turned into a triumphant success. The interest to us at the moment is that the Prince's own exhibit was the model houses for the labouring classes, of which we show the

FIG. 130.—The Doctor's Visit, 1821.   (After Cruikshank.)

FIG. 131.—Rosewood Piano of Six Octaves (1820) made
by Thomas Tomkison (working 1795-1825)
(*Bethnal Green Museum, London.*)

original engraving in Fig. 124, built near the south entrance
to the Exhibition. The model house consisted of four
dwellings—two up and two downstairs. Each dwelling
contained a general sitting-room and kitchen, two small
bedrooms (one for boys, and the other girls) and a large
bedroom for the parents and babies, a scullery and a
decent water-closet. All the rooms had cupboards, the
building was fireproof, and each had its own water supply.
The Prince was assisted by Mr. Roberts, the architect.
The cost was estimated at £440 to £480 for the block of
four, and the rental at 3s. 6d. to 4s. a week each.

After the Exhibition a similar block was built at the

FIG. 132.—Papier-Mâché Bed. English, about 1850.
(Given to the Bethnal Green Museum, London, by H.M. Queen Mary)

entrance to Kennington Park, in South London, and can
still be seen there. Strachey in his book raises the interesting point of what might have happened in England if the
Prince had not been cut off in his prime. This patient
German, with his high sense of duty and his love for
orderliness, gaining in experience and reputation as the
years passed, might have come to such a position of
authority that he would have been able to overcome the
inertia and lack of planning which is so noticeable a

FIG. 133.—Roasting Range, the Pavilion, Brighton.
(*Nash, Architect*, 1820.)

characteristic of the Englishman. Had the Consort lived
the cellar dwellings of Fig. 118 might not have disgraced
us at the present day.

Quite early among various efforts was the *Society for
Improving the Conditions of the Labouring Classes*, which

still carries on its work from a location in Bloomsbury. We find large blocks of working class flats erected about the mid-nineteenth century, e.g. round Drury Lane, with tablets saying they are due to such societies. They rendered valuable service, but of course standards of living and comfort have advanced vastly since then. These blocks of workers' flats later multiplied exceedingly, but many strongly individual workers prefer the old small terraced cottages with gardens, and grieve when they decay and are condemned. Now they are getting this type in the Pre-fabricated Houses as a temporary stopgap. The enormous rises in the cost of building have made difficult the task of providing convenient homes for workers and the older people now forming an increasing proportion of our population.

The other day we came across a charming folio of *Designs for Cottages and Schools* by John Hall, Secretary of the very Society mentioned above in 1825. There are pleasant coloured plates of Regency single and double cottages (Fig. 125), lodges, small farmhouses and schools, one a "School of Industry". The text is quaint and appealing, but they actually provided for constant hot water and similar amenities. Living rooms were to be 9 feet high and sleeping rooms 8 feet. There was to be a plot of $1\frac{1}{4}$ acres of land per cottage, with rents at 3s. a week, using a sort of concrete and our old friend, pisé de terre, or rammed earth, (which was revived after the 1914 war with varying results), stuccoed outside and whitewashed within. Costs were estimated at £143 to £184 for single and £260 to £330 for double cottages, according to the style and number built, about one fifth of present day figures.

FURNITURE.—We can now leave slums and consider the furniture of the early nineteenth century, which hitherto has received scant attention. It cannot of course compare with the eighteenth-century masterpieces of Chippendale, Hepplewhite and Sheraton; still it has a great interest of its own and was well made.

Take the family party scene of 1806 shown in Fig. 120;

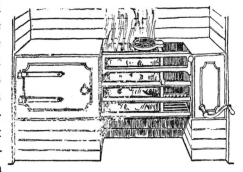

FIG. 134.—Thomas Robinson's Range (1780).

the polished steel grate and marble mantelpiece are quite simple and nice, and the glass over has Sphinx heads on its pilasters, with an admixture of Greek ornament. Napoleon's campaign in Egypt had advertised that country, and the sphinx became a popular decorative feature; you can see it again in the patterned borders on the walls. The chairs and sofa in Fig. 120 are in black with gold lines, and these colours are repeated in the carpet.

Another chair of the same type is shown in Fig. 122; again black and gold is used, but with little added red touches. It is a little bit too architectural for a chair, which should be so suave in its lines that it looks as if it had been shaped and not built. Fig. 123 is an amusing example of what we call "cow-hocked" chairs—that is, the type where the hind legs incline together at the back and are not so wide across the bottom as they are at the top. By the way, when drawing a chair see if this is so, because it adds complications to a difficult subject. This chair was made in beech grained to look like rosewood, which was now the fashionable wood.

Fig. 129 shows the brass inlay in the top rail of Fig. 123, with a Greek flavour in the design.

Brass inlays again appear on the rosewood piano (Fig. 131). The veneered borders with the grain of the wood applied crossways are pleasant, and the whole design is a successful treatment of a difficult subject. The bedroom in Fig. 130 is quite a homely room. Fig. 132 shows a bed which is an amazing piece of work. In the 'forties a fashion sprang up of japanned papier mâché, and

FIG. 135.—Early Nineteenth-Century Carron Range.

generally with a black ground on which were painted vividly-coloured flowers, and to heighten the general gaiety of the effect mother-of-pearl was inlaid as well. This treatment was applied to tea-trays, chairs and, as we have seen, beds. Fig. 132 must be seen to be believed, and fortunately this is possible by going to the Bethnal Green Museum. The canopy at the back is 8 feet high, and the fringe at the top is in green wool, and the cords and tassels in green and gold. The rep curtains are green bordered with green and gold. The bed is 6 feet 10 inches long and 4 feet 8 inches wide.

With this bed we come to an end of the history of English furniture. Chairs, tables and the rest of the household gear have been made and used since, but they are in a different category altogether. Made before 1851, as they approach old age they are felt to have earned a certain reverence, and so can be cherished as antiques;

FIG. 136.—The Bodley Range, A.D. 1802.

after 1851, and even before their coverings have been worn out, they become second-hand and are mocked at in the sale-rooms, and pass to the lodging-houses and apartments.

Figs. 126–128 show some of the furniture which was exhibited at the Great Exhibition of 1851, and so that there may be no deception we have reproduced the original engravings. What can be said for it? It carries on no tradition, but jumbles up all the styles. The Exhibition was a glorification of the machine, and the furniture was thrown in. In the same way the people who bought it and used it in their homes had been so busy acquiring wealth by the use of the machine that they had little time left for anything else. Their furniture had to have an atmosphere of richness about it and look as if the host of the party were really and truly affluent—not much else mattered.

COOKING.—To study this subject in a really regal way we will return to the Pavilion at Brighton, which we have already illustrated in Figs. 1 and 115.

Between the banqueting room (Fig. 1) and the kitchen

comes the table deckers' room, and its nice name explains its use.

The kitchen in the Pavilion is a fine place, 42 feet by 38 feet, with a lantern light in the ceiling supported by four iron columns disguised as palm trees, and provided with copper leaves at the top. On one side comes the great roasting range, as Fig. 133. This has a beautiful copper canopy over it to carry off the steam and smells into a flue in the chimney. There are other canopies as well over the marble pastry-making slabs at the sides, with dutch tiles at the back. The joints or birds to be roasted were put on to the spits as shown, and these, being placed in the grooves on the hinged arms, were turned by chains passing round pulley-wheels on the ends of the spits ; the chains at the upper ends passed over wooden pulley-wheels which are attached to the horizontal spindle, turned by bevel gears from a smoke vane in the chimney. This was, or still is, turned by the rising heat of the flue. On the other side of the kitchen is a hot plate. This has a furnace at one end, and a flue passes from this horizontally under the hot plate until it is taken up vertically in the wall behind, and here dampers are arranged to regulate the draught. Providing the vertical flue was high enough, sufficient draught would be made to draw the fire and heat along under the hot plate. This hot plate has every appearance of being as old as the range, and saucepans would have been heated over circular holes in the hot plate for making sauces. There are coppers in the adjoining vegetable kitchen, with the original covers engraved " P. R.," for the Prince Regent. The oven, or ovens, have disappeared in alterations which have been carried out in this part of the building, and this is a pity, as we should have been able to find out whether the Regent had introduced one of the new kitchen ranges which were being used at this time. There would certainly have been a brick oven for bread, but a range would have made a useful addition.

The earliest description of a range we have come across

ICE HOUSE AT ASHRIDGE HERTS.
LIKE A LARGE WELL COVERED BY A
BRICK VAULT, CUT OFF
BY VAULTED PASSAGE,
AS SECTION AT A, ALL
BUILT INTO THE HILLSIDE.

FIG. 137.—An Ice House.

is the specification of the range patented by Thomas
Robinson on October 21st, 1780. This says : " One side
of the fire is the oven, and the other side is made to wind
up with a cheeck. The top bar in front is made to fall
down occasionally to a level with the second bar. The
moving cheeck is made with a socket in it to receive a
swinging trivet. The oven is made of cast iron, nearly
square in front, the door hung with hinges and fastened
with a handle and a turnbuckle, and the oven is provided
with fillets for the shelves to rest upon. The oven must be
enclosed with bricks and mortar." The old roasting
ranges, as Fig. 133, had the cheeks which could be wound
up to reduce the size of the fire, so what Robinson did was
to add the oven at the side, which made the fitting much
more useful and suitable for the smaller houses which were
springing up in the suburbs of London and the industrial
towns. We show this range in Fig. 134.

The Robinson range developed into the nineteenth-
century open range, with a boiler added on the opposite

side to the oven, as Fig. 135. The setting of the oven was improved. In the Robinson range, Fig. 134, this was just set on brickwork, and the fire came against one side. In Fig. 135 the oven inside had a circular back, and in setting it the bottom of the oven was kept level with the fire bars, and a space was left under for hot air. A space was left as well on the left side and back of the oven into which this heated air could pass up from the bottom space out of the grating at A, Fig. 135. The oven was heated by the fire on its right-hand side, and conducting plates were cast on this to assist the passage of the hot air around the oven.

The range of bars to hold the fire had a sliding cheek to reduce its size, and a trivet to take the kettle. The boiler was returned around the back to get part of it near the fire ; it had to be filled by hand, and if this was forgotten then the boiler burnt out and was useless. Notwithstanding the hot-air chamber around the oven, it got much hotter on one side than the other, and to get over this its shelf was made to turn on a pivot, so that the food to be cooked could be turned to the heat. It was this open range which devoured coals and poured out the smoke that made the nineteenth-century London fogs. Fortunately for us we are beginning to forget what these were like. The late Sir Frederick Treves, a distinguished doctor of those days, estimated that in a fog in London a square mile of air contained 6 tons of soot, and killed people " not by scores and hundreds, but by thousands " ; as well that " the lungs of an adult dweller in big cities are dingy thunder-cloud blue in colour, due absolutely to dirt and soot in the atmosphere." Fig. 135 was one of the principal causes of all this.

The next step seems to have come about by trying to combine an oven with the hot plate ; the latter had shown that you could conduct heat in horizontal flues if you had a sufficiently high vertical chimney to create a draught. This is what the Bodley Range, as Fig. 136, which was patented on February 27th, 1802, aimed at. This seems to have been the first range or kitchener with a closed top. The fire was open in front, and could be used for roasting. The oven appears to have a fire-brick between it and the fire, so there was less danger of scorching, but the flue on the other three sides of the oven led to more equal heating. Still there was no provision as yet for diverting the oven heat so that this could come from the top for cooking meat, and the bottom for pastry. The flue, however, not only heated the oven, but the hot plate over it, so that the top of the range could be used for boiling. To do all this the fire-box had to be kept full up, and the coal consumption was as much as twelve to fifteen scuttles a day. All the kitcheners seem to have descended from the Bodley range.

It was Count Rumford (1753–1814) who invented the water-jacketed roasting pan, which kept down the temperature of the fat under the joint in the oven and so prevented it from spluttering over and being burnt, with unpleasant and smelly results. Rumford as well has a " roaster " to his credit ; this consisted of an oven in the form of a cylinder placed within another, the space between the two being the flue, with the furnace at the bottom and the chimney at the top. The roaster appears to have been a scientific toy which, though it pointed the way, did not come into general use.

Passing from heat to cold, Fig. 137 shows how ice was provided for cooling drinks and making ices in the early nineteenth century. The example shown still remains, and will remain until man or an earthquake destroys it, in the park of Ashridge, Hertfordshire, which we illustrate in Fig. 107, and it appears to be of the same date as the house (1806–13). This ice house is one more illustration of the cleverness with which the old people got over their difficulties, and the self-help which they practised. They could not make ice, so in the winter they cut it off the ponds and lakes and stored it underground as shown—first a layer of straw, then one of ice, and so on. Buried in the deep blackness of the vault, cut off from the outer air by the three doors in the entrance passage, and further insulated by being buried underground, the ice kept itself frozen until it was wanted in the summer. Please notice the ingenious arrangement by which, with sloping doors, a pulley-wheel was arranged in the brick vault of the passage, so that it could be used to haul up and lower ice in the ice house itself. While we were measuring in the passage one of the authors was nosing about with the one electric torch, and became interested in various stalactite forms on the ceiling; the other author, prone on tummy, with head over the edge, was attempting to judge the depth of vault by dropping pebbles into it, when the first, discovering that the stalactites were really bats, fled shrieking with the light and, banging the outer door to keep the bats in, left the second in velvet-black darkness. All this to sound a note of warning: when measuring an ice house take a bat-lover for an assistant.

LIGHTING.—In country houses people still had to depend on candles for lighting the reception rooms, with all the trouble of snuffing the candles and cleaning the candle-sticks. Lamps of the cruzie type, as shown in Fig. 30, were used in the kitchen and offices, and burning as they did animal and fish oils, or the contents of the frying-pan after the frying, they must have been smelly contraptions. Good colza oil lamps seem to have come in about 1836, and paraffin was first used for lighting about 1853. Boulton and Watt were the first to use gas to illuminate their works in 1803, and by 1810 it was being used for lighting the streets. There is a good tale told that when it was installed in the House of Commons members were seen going round feeling the pipes to see if they were hot. They were afraid the flame continued down the pipes.

GAS COOKING.—We cannot discover when gas cooking was first introduced, but gas cookers were exhibited at the 1851 Exhibition.

And now, having come to the end of the space allotted for early nineteenth-century building and furnishing, may we make a suggestion ? If our readers will familiarize themselves with the general characteristics of buildings so that they can date them, they can then apply such knowledge to the town or district in which they live. There may be an old castle, as in Fig. 3, with the remains of the township which grew up around it in the Middle Ages. The mills may be there which were mentioned in Doomsday, and a school of 1541 show the Tudor interest in education. Almost certainly there will be pleasant Stuart and Georgian houses, and Regency ones like those we have illustrated in this book. Industrial and Suburban developments can be noted, and the nearest Grid lines will bring the survey up to date.

In this way the town will come to life and form the background of history, because history can be shown by bricks and mortar, as well as found in the printed pages of books.

Lady with child and cradle.
Greek revival style.

By Henry Moses, 1825.

CHAPTER VIII

NINETEENTH-CENTURY CLOTHING

THE clothing trade was destined to be one of the chief instruments of the commercial expansion of the nineteenth century. Great industrial centres were to spring up in Lancashire and Yorkshire, and the materials woven on the looms there were sent all over the world. These were paid for either by the importation of raw materials or foodstuffs for the population of the industrial towns.

There was nothing very revolutionary about the period, and the inventors contented themselves with perfecting the ideas of Kay, Hargreaves, Arkwright, Crompton and Cartwright, of whom we wrote in Chapter III. Improvements were made in detail, and one of the most important of these was the introduction of the Jacquard apparatus, which made the weaving of elaborate patterns very much simpler than it had been.

If we turn back to Fig. 47, of the hand loom, we shall find that patterns were possible by introducing colours in the weft. If a black thread were used, for example, and this was passed under and over the warp threads, like darning, you got a pattern, and this could be varied by going under three and over one, and so on. This was, and still is, the only way to achieve pattern, the interlacing of different coloured threads. In all textile designing the patterns should be built up on squares representing crossing threads.

We saw how in Fig. 47 the warp threads were lifted or lowered so that the shuttle could be passed through the shed by being attached to loops in the healds, and how

FIG. 138.—Power Loom (1851).
(*Science Museum, London.*)

FIG. 139.—Original Singer Sewing Machine
(1854).
(*Science Museum, London.*)

FIG. 140.—Spinning, Reeling and Boiling the Yarn in Northern
Ireland, 1791.

By W. Hincks.

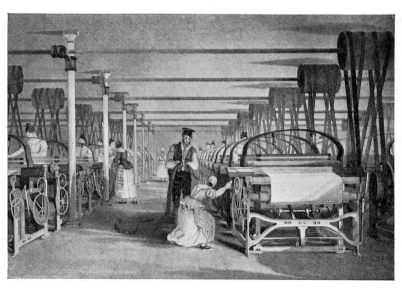

FIG. 141.—Power Loom Weaving, *c.* 1835.

By Sir E. Baines.

FIG. 142.—Upsetting the Charlies, 1821.

these were operated by being connected to treadles. So complicated patterns meant more healds and more treadles, and the work was consequently very skilled. This did not suit nineteenth-century ideas at all; they wanted mass production. The Jacquard apparatus was a step in this direction. Figs. 49 and 148 explain this.

Jacquard seems to have made a commercial success in France, in 1804, of inventions of Falcon in 1728, and Vaucanson in 1745, and it was introduced into this country early in the nineteenth century. Fig. 148 explains the principle. The Jacquard apparatus could be applied to the hand-loom where it was retained, see Fig. 47A, or used in conjunction with the power loom.

On p. 72 we described how the power loom was invented by Cartwright in 1785. This was improved in detail, not principle, and Fig. 138 shows how far the designers had got by 1851. At first sight it appears a very complicated bit of machinery, but after a little study it will be found to be only a mechanical version of Fig. 47. The machine, competing against the human hand, asks for and has to take endless trouble. We explain the mechanical principle in Fig. 149.

Comparing Fig. 138 with the hand loom, Fig. 47, and Kay's flying shuttle, Fig. 53, we can see how the various parts of these were incorporated in the power loom. On Fig. 138, starting from the back, the warp threads can be seen at A, the healds at B, and heald shafts at C; the batten is seen at D, with the reed at E, and the shed at F,

FIG. 143.—Boxing. (After Cruikshank.)

with the shuttle just entering it. G shows the picker, which

FIG. 144.—Fencing. (After Cruikshank.)

FIG. 145.—Fly-Fishing in 1831.   (After James Pollard.)
(The Gade, Water End, Hertfordshire.)

FIG. 146.—The Dance.
(After Cruikshank.)

throws the shuttle out of its box through the shed by means of the picking stick H and strap connections, and the cloth when woven passes on to the cloth beam I. The principle is just the same as the hand loom plus Kay's shuttle. For pattern work a Jacquard apparatus was fixed over this.

SEWING MACHINES. —It was not to be expected that sewing —one of the oldest of the arts—would escape the attention of the inventors. The history of sewing goes back into the remotest antiquity. There is, in a case on the left-hand gallery as you enter, in the Prehistoric Room at the British Museum a small cardboard box, the contents of which we illustrated in Fig. 54 of our book on the Old Stone Age. It contains the apparatus for making the bone needles which men then used for sewing skins together. First an awl was made which punched a hole through which the sinew could be passed ; next came a kind of crotchet needle, which pulled it through, and then a needle with a pierced eye through which the sinew could be threaded ; the needle started life then as an awl, and the principle of sewing was established in Solutrean times. Steel needles were probably

FIG. 147.—The Quadrille, 1821. (After Cruikshank).

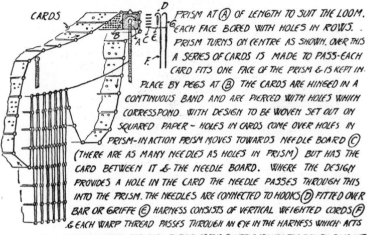

CARDS

PRISM AT (A) OF LENGTH TO SUIT THE LOOM. EACH FACE BORED WITH HOLES IN ROWS. . PRISM TURNS ON CENTRE AS SHOWN. OVER THIS A SERIES OF CARDS IS MADE TO PASS-EACH CARD FITS ONE FACE OF THE PRISM & IS KEPT IN PLACE BY PEGS AT (B) THE CARDS ARE HINGED IN A CONTINUOUS BAND AND ARE PIERCED WITH HOLES WHICH CORRESPOND WITH DESIGN TO BE WOVEN SET OUT ON SQUARED PAPER ~ HOLES IN CARDS COME OVER HOLES IN PRISM-IN ACTION PRISM MOVES TOWARDS NEEDLE BOARD (C) (THERE ARE AS MANY NEEDLES AS HOLES IN PRISM) BUT HAS THE CARD BETWEEN IT & THE NEEDLE BOARD. WHERE THE DESIGN PROVIDES A HOLE IN THE CARD THE NEEDLE PASSES THROUGH THIS INTO THE PRISM. THE NEEDLES ARE CONNECTED TO HOOKS (D) FITTED OVER BAR OR GRIFFE (E) HARNESS CONSISTS OF VERTICAL WEIGHTED CORDS (F) & EACH WARP THREAD PASSES THROUGH AN EYE IN THE HARNESS WHICH ACTS AS THE HEALD. THERE IS A CARD FOR EACH THROW OF THE SHUTTLE. WHERE THE DESIGN DOES NOT PROVIDE A HOLE IN THE CARD THE HOOKS ARE PUSHED OFF GRIFFE AS (G) & HARNESS DOES NOT ACT.

FIG. 148.—The Mechanical Principle of the Jacquard Apparatus.
See Fig. 47A.

introduced into England in the sixteenth century, and with them most beautiful work was done at the rate of about thirty stitches a minute. The inventors thought this was much too slow, and at the end of the eighteenth

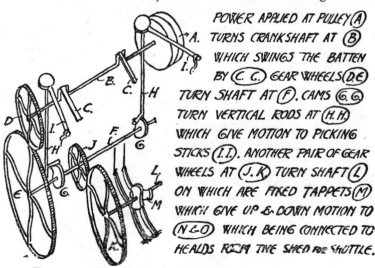

POWER APPLIED AT PULLEY (A) A. TURNS CRANKSHAFT AT (B) WHICH SWINGS THE BATTEN BY (C.C.) GEAR WHEELS (D.E) TURN SHAFT AT (F). CAMS (G.G) TURN VERTICAL RODS AT (H.H.) WHICH GIVE MOTION TO PICKING STICKS (I.I.). ANOTHER PAIR OF GEAR WHEELS AT (J.K) TURN SHAFT (L) ON WHICH ARE FIXED TAPPETS (M) WHICH GIVE UP & DOWN MOTION TO (N & O) WHICH BEING CONNECTED TO HEALDS FORM THE SHED FOR SHUTTLE.

FIG. 149.—The Mechanical Principle of the Power Loom
on Fig. 138.

century they got to work. Elias Howe, in 1845, designed the first lock-stitch machine using a threaded needle and shuttle. If you take your mother's machine (with her permission) and turn it by hand very slowly you will find that the needle pauses in its stroke, which causes a loop to form in the cotton, and the threaded shuttle goes through this, and then the needle pursues its course and pulls the thread tight.

FIG 150.—Pelisse, Mantelet, 1803.

It was in 1851 that I. M. Singer patented his first sewing machine, which is now at the Science Museum, London, and which we illustrate in Fig. 139. It is still in working order, and if any of our readers go to the Museum we suggest that they ask Mr. E. J. Taylor, the chief attendant in the Textile Gallery, to open the case so that the noise of this early machine can be properly appreciated ; at the same time Mr. Taylor might be persuaded to give a demonstration on the power loom (Fig. 138) Here we should like to return thanks to him for his kind assistance in elucidating the mysteries of his textile machinery.

DRESS.—We can now turn to the dress which was made of the materials woven on the looms and find out how it reflected the spirit of the times, and this is at once

FIG. 151.—The Tailor, 1821.
(After Cruikshank.)

apparent. At the very end of the eighteenth century, when " Romantic " houses like Ashridge were being built, as Fig. 107, the people had to have " Romantic " clothes. The women wore large hats, with flowing curls, and loose frills at the neck. And here is an interesting point which mystifies one author, but is quite feasible to the other. One would have imagined that the position of women's waists was settled when women were designed; but this was not the case in the nineteenth century; sometimes waists went up, sometimes they went down. As the dress became less formal the waist-line rose, heels were flatter, and less stiff silk and more muslin, calico and chintz was worn. Fine embroidery, though, was used to decorate the materials.

Between 1804 and 1808 a modified classical dress was worn, and the waist-line rose to under the arms (see the first lady in Fig. 155). The hair was cut short and dressed in small ringlets, or frizzed, or worn with a straight fringe on the forehead. Sometimes real flowers were worn in the hair, and the bonnets were modelled on Grecian helmets.

In the eighteenth century pockets were worn under the skirts, outside the petticoats; in the beginning of the nineteenth, women carried bags which they called

" indispensables." Parasols, sometimes hinged, as Fig. 155, had been carried since the last quarter of the eighteenth century. The poke bonnet seems to have developed from the helmet shape; it was small in 1815, enormous by 1827, and survived until 1860. Hats also were very large and over-trimmed in 1828, and were parodied by Cruikshank, together with tiny waists (see second lady, Fig. 155).

FIG. 152.—Walking Dress, 1821.

From about 1808 the waist-line (in women) gradually dropped, until in 1820 to 1830 it had reached the lowest level, but it was very tight, and the skirts very full.

We must confess that we are very interested in this waist-line problem. What did it reflect ? Was it economical, political or psychological ? Here is a subject beyond two poor artists and far more suitable for the real scholar.

FIG. 153.—The Riders, 1821.

Hair had become long again by 1821, and was worn high with fantastic bows and curls. High tortoise-shell combs can be noted in 1830 fashion plates. In 1836 hair was plaited in wickerwork fashion on the crown of the head and flowers inserted for the evening. Sleeves to the wrist had been worn for day wear since 1804, and they grew larger as the waist-line

FIG. 154.—Young Man, 1821.
(After Cruikshank.)

dropped, and became enormous in 1830. By 1841 they were tight again in the upper arm; the bodice was pointed, the waist still small, and the skirt full.

In 1845 the hair was worn with a simple middle parting and side bunches of curls, as third lady, Fig. 155. Shoes throughout the first half of the century were of thin leather, often of slipper shape, with little if anything which would be called a heel to-day.

The full skirt question is important. If you go to the museums and study the early nineteenth-century dresses you will find that they are all on the small side. The women were tiny, and that was all right when they were young and fairy-like, but it was all wrong when they became middle-aged and portly. We regret to have to use the latter word, but in the cause of historical research it must be employed. The full skirt remained until 1854, when it became fuller still by the use of the crinoline introduced from Paris. Made first of stiff horsehair and then of steel hoops, it was spoken of as a hygienic contrivance which enabled the skirt to be so large that the waist, by comparison, seemed small, and that without the undue compression which had been used till then. It was

FIG. 155.—Costume in the First Half of the Nineteenth Century.

a contrivance which brought comfort to the middle-aged and kept them in the fashion, and as the young girl can wear anything and look nice, everybody was happy. To sum up, you can say that simplicity was the key-note of the early part of the century, with ex-travagance at the end of the Regent's time, regaining a measure of simplicity by 1850 under good Queen Vic-toria. The three groups in Fig. 155 show these three periods.

FIG. 156.—The Parson and His Wife, 1821. (After Cruikshank.)

So far as men were concerned, their waist-line does not seem to have troubled them. In the late eighteenth century knee-breeches had descended to mid-calf for daily use, and shoes were tied instead of buckled, and by 1816 pantaloons of stockinette to ankle, with black silk socks and pumps, were worn for the evening. The broad-brimmed Napoleonic hats took the place of the three-cornered ones, and in the early nineteenth century the crowns of these rose and, though varying in shape, the top-hat arrived. Men wore their own hair, cut short, and their faces were clean-shaven. Their collars stood up on each side of their faces, and they wore black cravats.

In 1825 broadcloth great-coats were used for travelling, without capes, and in this year Charles Macintosh intro-duced waterproofing, and soon after mackintoshes came into use for wet weather. By 1825 breeches had become

FIG. 157.—Riding Dress, 1832.

trousers, fastened with straps under the instep, and by 1830 black ones were worn in the evening, though knee breeches and *chapeau bras* continued in use for Court and the opera.

By 1830 the tops of men's sleeves were very full, and gathered and pleated at the armhole. The coat, with high collar and spreading lapels, was worn well open to show the satin

waistcoat, tight at the waist, over wide-topped trousers, diminishing down to small ankles, as first man in Fig. 155. The coats were usually of coloured cloth, cut away with tails, and the trousers of white or coloured nankeen. Low shoes were worn until 1825, with riding boots to the knee for walking.

By 1841 the cravats were still dark, and covered the shirt front and collar, with a white slip between cravat and waistcoat, as second man, Fig. 155.

Whiskers began to be worn, and by 1855 moustaches were allowed to grow. These, the sign of ferocity, had hitherto been regarded as a privilege of the military. Trousers became tight, and sleeves as well. The skirted frock-coat was usual, although these,

FIG. 158.—Dressing-Gown, 1839.

196

FIG. 159.—A small Merry-go-round in a Village, *c.* 1810.

By W. H. Pyne.

FIG. 160.—Children dancing in the grounds of a Country House,
c. 1820.

FIG. 161.—The Smithfield Horse Show, c. 1825.

with military frogging, had been worn as early as 1825;
the coat had a stand-up collar. We should like to give
our readers another reminder here, that fine collections of
early nineteenth-century clothes can be seen at the Victoria
and Albert, the Bethnal Green, and the London Museums,
in London.

A Card Party.

By Henry Moses, 1825.

CHAPTER IX

THE SUBSIDIARY TRADES: TRANSPORT

IT IS doubtful if we ought to consider Transport as subsidiary; Rudyard Kipling in some of his later stories is fond
of the dictum: "Transportation is Civilisation." Anyhow
transport was certainly the most important of the subsidiary
trades in England in the nineteenth century. It was to alter
the face of the countryside and impinge on its life in a
hundred different ways. At the beginning of the century
the roads were coming into their own once more ; then these
were to be forgotten and again have a later renaissance when
the motor-car came along. Roads are pleasant things, and
what more delightful occupation is there on a winter's
evening than to take out your maps and trace one's
journeys on the roads of England ? And they vary—the
Roman road, which thrusts its purposeful way over the
countryside, and the winding lanes between the villages,
which started as the tracks between the common fields.

There is no greater tribute to the Roman genius than
the road system which the Romans laid out when they
came to Britain, and which we still use. Imagine the
difficulties of foreseeing exactly the line on which trade
and inter-town communication would follow, to look ahead
nearly 2000 years. The Romans were great planners.

We have seen in what state Celia Fiennes found the
roads in the seventeenth century. They were improved
by the Turnpike Trusts of the eighteenth century, and then
at the end of the eighteenth and the beginning of the
nineteenth Macadam and Telford got to work. They
dug down to the foundations of the Roman roads, cleared
out the pot-holes and brought the main roads into fine
condition, so that the mail-coaches could run at an average
and unheard of speed of eight miles an hour, with bursts
of eleven to twelve.

Fig 162.—Royal Mail Coach (1820) at the Science Museum, London.

But the good macadam road was a very different thing from those we have now. Boys and girls who read this book will hardly remember the roads which were general when their parents were young. The surface was worn off by the iron tyres of the wheels—because rubber was not used as it is now—and laid on the top of the road in a good solid layer of dust. By May all the hedgerows along the roads were white; if you bicycled in breeches and stockings there was a pattern of dirt on your legs where the dust had blown through. The first motors raced along and left behind them uncurling serpentine clouds of dust, and the people you passed by fled or, holding handkerchiefs over their noses, glared at you. The horse is the only sufferer by the tarred roads, and we have forgotten what dust and mud can be like.

The bridge-builders continued their work, and the Menai Bridge was designed by Thomas Telford in 1819, and opened in 1826. The engineers could have had very little data to guide them as to the stresses set up by a living load, but they were plucky and inspired and achieved the factors of safety. This is especially true of some of the earliest railway viaducts—nobody had ever run a train over a bridge before (Fig. 74).

VEHICLES.—When we come to vehicles pride of place must be given to the Mail Coach (Fig. 32), and Fig. 162 shows an actual example which can be seen at the Science Museum, in London. This dates from about 1820, or the heyday of coaching. The front wheels are 38 inches diameter, back wheels 48 inches, with a wheel-base of 6 feet 6 inches. The under-framing is much the same as the timber carriage, Fig. 98, with a pole or perch between the front and back axles. On this under-carriage the coach body is fixed by springs. The coach carried four persons inside, the driver and one passenger beside him, and four others on the seat behind, with the guard over the boot with his blunderbuss in front of him for the highwaymen. The coach was drawn by four horses.

FIG. 163.—Steam Omnibus, Coach and Waggon, *c.* 1835.

FIG. 164.—Gurney's Steam Coach, London to Bath, *c.* 1835.

FIG. 165.—Early Train, drawn by the primitive "Novelty" Locomotive, with Omnibus and owners' Coaches.

FIG. 166.—The " North Star " and Train of early Carriages.

FIG. 167.—Steam Omnibus, Edinburgh to Leith, c. 1860.

The best description we know of a coach ride is the one in " Tom Brown's Schooldays," which, though it was published in 1857, deals with the period when Tom first went to Rugby, about 1837—that is, just at the end of the great coaching period, when the railways were beginning to drive the coaches off the road. Tom comes up from the Vale the day before with his father, and they stay the night at the Peacock Inn, Islington, so as to catch the Tally-ho for Leicester. Tom has beef-steak with oyster sauce for supper, and drinks brown stout. As the coach leaves Islington at 3 a.m., Tom is called at 2.30, and has a three-hours' drive, on the top, before dawn. Just as we have forgotten dust, we cannot remember now how cold it could be driving in an open carriage. But the Tally-ho is a tip-top goer and averages ten miles an hour, and Tom experiences the thrill, which we all do, of driving along at night when the world is asleep. Then the dawn comes, and the world wakes up and the road comes to life, and appetite as well, but this is stayed by a twenty-minutes' halt at an inn famous for its breakfasts. Pigeon pie, ham, cold boiled beef, kidneys, steak, bacon and eggs, buttered toast and muffins is the fare offered to Tom.

Fig. 168 shows the first omnibus introduced into England by G. Shillibeer, a coach-builder. Two started to run on July 4th, 1829, between *The Yorkshire Stingo*, public house, Marylebone Road, and the Bank, in London, and the fare was 1s. Each omnibus carried twenty-two passengers inside and was drawn by three horses.

This led to the introduction of a steam omnibus. In *The Times* of April 25th, 1833, an account was given of one that started running then from Paddington to the Bank. It was stated that " there can be no possibility of explosion," and " the guide, who sits in front, has complete control, and can arrest its progress instantaneously." Starting at six miles an hour, when it cleared the crowd " the velocity was increased to the rate of ten miles an hour." The authorities, however, refused to license " the

FIG. 168.—Shillibeer's Omnibus, 1829.
(*Model in Science Museum, London.*)

Enterprise Steam Coach," so it died the death. This was
built by Hancock, but Gurney designed one to run between
London and Bath (Fig. 164). We wonder if the varied
steam vehicles of Fig. 163 ever ran.

We illustrated a post-chaise, perch-phaeton and a gig
in Vol. II., and the two first, with the Victorian landau,
were suspended by springs over an under-framing like the
timber carriage. It was the brougham, as Fig. 170, which
introduced the new principle of building a rigid body and
attaching the springs and wheels to this, without the
connecting pole or perch. The specimen at the Science
Museum is the original built for Lord Chancellor Brougham
by Messrs. Robinson and Cook in 1838. It created a great
sensation then and remained in use until the motor-car age.

Joseph Hansom, the architect, designed his cab in 1834,
but this did not resemble the hansom which became very
popular during the nineteenth century.

Unfortunately we can only deal with beginnings, but
space must be found for the hobby horse, as Fig. 176,

FIG. 169.—Market Day outside the Old " Red Lion " at Greenwich.

By Thomas Rowlandson.

introduced into England from France in 1818, when it was described as a " Pedestrian Curricle." Hobby horses became all the rage, and there are old prints of the period showing the schools where you could learn to ride them. Round and round the riders go before their admiring friends, and some of the greatly daring ones actually lift both legs off the ground, and so experience the thrill of balancing in a spread-eagled fashion. This discovery that it was possible to balance yourself and progress on two wheels led to the early bicycle of 1839, as Fig. 180. This was designed by Kirkpatrick Macmillan, a blacksmith of Courthill, Dumfriesshire, and the propulsion by treadles and cranks is very ingenious. It was really in advance of the " boneshaker " of 1868, but, on the other hand, you could not have turned at all sharply without fouling your feet against the wheel. Probably to go straight ahead was quite thrilling enough. Any readers who are interested should go to the Science Museum, where there is a fine collection of early cycles, all dated, so that their development can be traced.

RAILWAY LOCOMOTIVES.—Actually there were railways long before there were locomotives. A print of 1754 shows stone from the quarries at Bath being transported in low trucks whose wheels run on rails. This was long before man invented the locomotive, which derived its name from *locus*, place, and *motio*, motion, because it performed the miracle of moving itself from place to place. Hitherto man had never been able to make anything which moved itself. His ships depended on the wind, and his coaches on the horse. Watt's steam engine puffed and grunted but stayed put, which was perhaps just as well.

Puffing Billys and the Rockets of a little later must have been bad to meet on the road, but imagination refuses to conceive what a Watt's locomotive would have been like. We often watch the behemoth at the Science Museum in action ; the great beams rock, the gears grind round, and it really does puff and grunt. Originally

FIG. 170.—The Original Brougham (1838).
(*Science Museum, London.*)

working at a very low pressure of 4 or 5 lb. per square inch, owing to the risk of explosion with the badly-made boilers of the time, it is not at all lively (Fig. 171).

It was Richard Trevithick (1771–1833) who altered all this by introducing a boiler which worked to a pressure of over 100 lb., and once this was done movement was suggested. Trevithick, who was the son of a Cornish mine manager, was born at Camborne, in Cornwall, so that during his boyhood he was to be much in touch with things mechanical. In 1797, when he was twenty-six, he had made the model of a road locomotive which can be seen at the Science Museum, London, and we illustrate this in Fig. 172. That it is only a model makes no difference to the fact that it was and is a locomotive possessing the power to move itself. True it only ran around Trevithick's table, but that does not matter ; imagine what your own feelings would have been had you been Trevithick.

The next step was the completion, on Christmas Eve, 1801, of a steam carriage to run on the roads, and the Dictionary of National Biography says that this carriage

FIG. 172.—Trevithick's Road Locomotive
Model, c. 1800.

(*Science Museum, London.*)

FIG. 171.—Boulton and Watt's Rotative Engine (1797).

(*Science Museum, London.*)

FIG. 173.—Davidson's, 1842, the first to run on a railway.

FIG. 174.—Farmer's Model Electric Train, 1847, from the inventor's reconstruction for the Chicago Fair, 1893 (*see p.* 219).

FIG. 175.—Cotton's Electro-magnetic Locomotive, 1846 (*see p.* 219).

EARLY ELECTRO-MAGNETIC LOCOMOTIVES.

conveyed the first load of passengers ever moved by the force of steam. We should say that this was rather a risky statement. Cugnot had experimented with a traction engine in 1770, and a model of his machine is preserved at the Conservatoire des Arts et Métiers, Paris. There is another model of Murdoch's locomotive in the Birmingham Art Gallery; this dates from 1781–86, and Oliver Evans's was at work in Philadelphia.

Whether these moved passengers or not we do not know, but Trevithick's did, and was known as the " Puffing Devil "; unfortunately it was burnt out while Trevithick and his friends were in an inn celebrating the success of this first run. 1803 saw another steam carriage, and then in February, 1804, Trevithick produced the first railway locomotive. This hauled 10 tons of iron and seventy men, in five waggons, at nearly five miles an hour for nine and a half miles over the rails used by the horse trams in the mines at Penydarran, near Merthyr Tydvil, South Wales.

Trevithick must have been possessed of humour, because in 1808 he brought a new locomotive to London, hired some land near Euston, put up a circular track and fenced it in, and charged 1s. a head for joy-rides at fifteen miles an hour (see Fig. 177).

The engine was called " Catch-me-who-can " and was backed to beat any horse running at Newmarket.

It will be well for any young Trevithick who may read these pages to take stock of the state of affairs which is revealed by the recital of achievement and dates which we have given above. Had the people had eyes to see, from the very moment at which Trevithick made his little model run round the table they might have foreseen the possibilities of his invention; had they had imagination they might have realized the enormous importance of the invention and the changes it was to make, not only in running around our little island, but in crossing the continents of the Old and New Worlds. This iron horse was destined to drive all the other horses off the road.

FIG. 176.—The Hobby Horse (1818).
(*Science Museum, London.*)

Surveyors had to go before it, spy out the land, scheme the gradients and make ready the way. The descendants of the navvies who had made the canals had a bigger task than their forebears and followed on the trail to dig and embank, and when the rails could not be taken over the mountains they had to tunnel through them. The engineers made the bridges, the iron-founders the rails, the builders the stations. New towns were to arise, and old ones which were passed by dwindled away. Man could peddle his goods over a continually expanding area, and trade and industry were to be revolutionized. The very character of the country was altered because men lost the road sense, and towns became a congeries of houses grouped around railway stations. All this was hidden from the riders in " Catch-me-who-can."

Trevithick seems to have exercised his inventive genius as well on steam-boats, dredgers and threshers. Any

FIG. 177.—Trevithick's ' Catch-me-who-can ' on the Site of Euston
Square, London (1809).

By Thomas Rowlandson.

FIG. 178.—A G.W.R. "single-wheeler" Locomotive, *c.* 1845, of the earlier
Broad Gauge Type, which ran (with eight wheels) till 1892.

By J. C. Bourne.

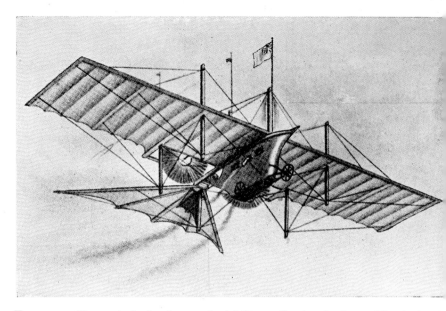

FIG. 179.—Henson's design for an 'Aerial Steam Carriage', 1842-3. The design for an aeroplane which was publicized the world over, and which led to widespread research and experiment

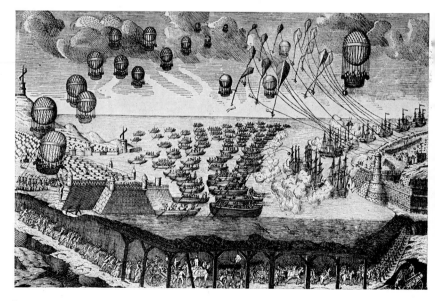

FIG. 179A.—A French dream of the invasion of England, c. 1805. The French forces invade by balloon and tunnel, and the English fly armed single-seater kites in defence

problem attracted him, and then about 1816 he went to Peru, made a fortune there, lost it in a revolution, and came back some years later to find that others had benefited by his work. Blenkinsop and Hedley had followed in his tracks with colliery locomotives, and then George Stephenson (1781–1848) appeared on the scene. He had been appointed engine-wright at the Killingworth Colliery in 1812, and began his experiments in 1813, and completed his first engine in 1814. This work led to him being appointed, in 1822, engineer to the Stockton and Darlington Railway, which had started the year before and was the first public steam railway to be made in the world; but it was only employed for carrying goods. A new Act of Parliament was obtained in 1823, authorizing the railway to carry passengers as well, but railways as we understand them had not yet come into being. The Liverpool and Manchester Railway was authorized in 1826, and when it was approaching completion in 1829 the directors, wishing to be quite sure that they were on the right side, appointed Messrs. Rastrick and Walker to visit all existing railways and report on the respective merits of locomotives or stationary engines drawing the trains by cables! Their report was rather in favour of the latter method of traction. The directors, however, very wisely determined to have a competition, and offered a prize of £500 for the best locomotive, and this led to the Rainhill trials, nine miles from Liverpool, on October 6th, 1829, at which the "Rocket" won the prize, and the "also rans" were the "Novelty," "Sans Pareil" and others. The locomotive had at last come into its own, thirty-two years since Trevithick's little model, Fig. 172, had run round the table and settled the principles. The world went railway mad. The "Best Friend" made its first trip in the U.S.A. on January 15th, 1831.

To return to the subject of our sketch, Trevithick on his return was not able to take his place again. Whether he had lost courage or the spark of his genius had died out

FIG. 180.—Macmillan Bicycle (1839).
(*Science Museum, London.*)

we cannot say, but he died in poverty and was buried in a
grave for poor persons at the parish church of Dartford,
in Kent, in 1833. He does not seem to have been esteemed
in his own time, but the wheel has turned full circle and in
1933 the centenary of his death was commemorated by
an exhibition of his work at the Science Museum in London,
and the Bishop of Rochester conducted a memorial service
at the Dartford church where he lies buried. Hence
our warning to young Trevithicks of to-day: it takes time
to knock ideas into the heads of Englishmen; the inventors may not be esteemed, and somebody else will make
the money, but the wheel turns, and in a hundred years
you are honoured and bishops praise you as a famous man.

But what is still more pleasant is that the celebrations
of his fellow-countrymen were forestalled by the action of
two American gentlemen, F. R. Low, the President of the
American Society of Mechanical Engineers, New York, and

FIG. 181.—View of Whampoa. Canton River, China, showing on the right the East Indiaman *Waterloo*, of 1315 tons, built in 1816 and broken up in 1834.

the Editor of *Power*, and R. C. Beadle, the Assistant President of International Combustion Engineering Corporation, New York, and editor of *Combustion*, who caused a tablet to be erected in the church at Dartford, setting out the facts we have given, in July, 1924.

STEAMBOATS.—While the locomotive engineers were at work others were experimenting with the application of the steam engine to water transport. The first practical steamboat seems to have been the *Charlotte Dundas*, made by Symington in 1801 for use on the Forth and Clyde Canal. In 1815 steamers appeared on the Thames. Then they began to be used for coasting and cross-Channel work, and gradually the voyages became longer. The Peninsular Steam Navigation Company was founded in 1837, and they bought the wooden paddle steamer, the *William Fawcett*, as Fig. 183, which had been built in 1829, and started running between Falmouth and Gibraltar, calling at ports between. In 1840 they extended their line to Egypt, later India and the Far East, and became the Peninsular & Oriental Steam Navigation Co.

It was not till 1838 that steamers began to sail regularly across the Atlantic. The paddle steamer *Sirius* began then, and took nineteen days, and ninety-four passengers. She was 178 feet long by 25.6 feet broad by 18 feet deep.

To go back to the *William Fawcett*, the length on deck was 74.3 feet, breadth 15.1 feet, and depth 8.4 feet. In fact, she could not have been very much bigger than the " penny steamers " which used to run on the Thames when we were children. These were paddle steamboats, with a funnel so arranged that it could be lowered when going under a bridge. The steamers had their own bridges, on which the captain walked and looked very nautical. The mate threw the mooring ropes to the men on the piers, and they attended to the gangways. Below decks were the engineers and engines, all working visibly and distilling an excellent odour into the air—something compounded of water, oil and steam, which was redolent to us of the ocean. It was a wonderful trip to zigzag down the Thames from Chelsea to Greenwich—let no one say they have seen London if they have not seen it from the Thames—and then below bridges, in the Pool, were real sea-going boats with the brine dripping off them.

Now the war is over there is a service of " River Buses " with a number of other boats, so that it is possible to go by steamer again from Westminster to Greenwich, and we hope you will all do it. Other steamers will take you from Westminster up the river to Hampton Court or Richmond but no boat goes right through London, and the unknown, shadowy, but all-powerful and narrow-minded authorities refuse to allow the little steamers to go on beyond Greenwich to Barking, when it really gets interesting past the docks. Paddle steamers, however, are, with a new screw one, again running from London Bridge to Southend, Margate and Clacton.

Our penny steamers were well enough for the Thames, but we should hardly have liked to cross the Bay of Biscay in them, or for that matter the *William Fawcett*, as Fig. 183. Nevertheless, we hear that later one Thames steamer was sold to someone in the Balkans and they managed to make the voyage out to there.

The *Great Britain* was the first screw steamer to cross the Atlantic, and this she did in fifteen days in 1845. She was as well the first large ship to be built of iron. The Americans, with their magnificent inland waterways, were ahead of us in steamship design. Robert Fulton's first successful steamer, the *Clermont*, was running on the Hudson in 1807, and Stevens had preceded him with a screw-driven boat. English design, however, produced an amazing *tour de force* in the *Great Eastern*, designed by Scott Russell and Isambard K. Brunel, the famous G.W.R. engineer, launched in 1858. She was nearly 700 feet long and her dimensions were not exceeded until 1899. She had six masts, and was propelled both by screw and paddle wheels; she cost £640,000 to build. She had a

Fig. 182.—The *Cutty Sark* (1869) 921 tons, in Falmouth Harbour, from under her own Bows.

FIG. 183.—The First P. & O., the *William Fawcett* (1829).
(*Model in Science Museum, London.*)

record of consistent bad luck, and after helping on the
Atlantic cable laying was broken up. (*V.* account in Vol.
IV, E.D.T.)

SAILING SHIPS.—This heading seems a little out of
place, coming after steamships. One might have imagined
that immediately the steamer was invented the sailing ship
would have been abandoned ; but this was not the case.
There was some sentiment in the contest ; a sailing ship
is one of the most beautiful things invented by man, and
so long as it did not spell absolute ruin there were men who
would send them sailing for the love of it. In the first part
of the nineteenth century it was the ambition of the captain
to become the owner of a ship, and then, if successful, others
would be bought and a small line or fleet founded. Captain
John Willis, who gave the order for building the *Cutty Sark*,
as Fig. 182, came of just such stock. His father had
started as a captain and built ships out of his savings, and
the son, John, had sailed his father's ships until he succeeded
to the business. So the salt of the sea was in his blood,
and when he built the *Cutty* as late as 1869, it was as

FIG. 184.—The *Joseph Cunard*, a barque of 680 tons, built probably about 1830. She traded between Liverpool and New Orleans, and was making voyages to India for a Scottish firm as late as 1844.

a sailing ship. The designer was Hercules Linton, who had just started ship-building with a partner called Scott. The *Cutty's* length is 212 feet 6 inches, breadth 36 feet, depth 21 feet, and she turned out to be a wonderful ship. That is one of the extraordinary things about shipbuilding —you can build two ships to the same plans and specification, and one will sail much better than the other. Given a good wind the *Cutty* could outsail most of the steamers of her day; they had to be content with eleven to twelve knots, while the *Cutty* was capable of seventeen to seventeen and a half knots, and on several occasions did 363 miles in the twenty-four hours. Such performances, however, could not have been obtained unless the man in command had been a fine seaman.

In course of time the machine won, and the *Cutty* fell on evil days and was sold to the Portuguese; they re-rigged her as a barquentine and painted false ports on her sides, as shown in the drawing of her bows in Fig. 182. Time passed, and then it happened that the *Cutty* sailed into Falmouth Harbour round about 1922, and though she did not know it Falmouth was to be for a time a haven of refuge for her. Captain Wilfred Dowman, a retired master mariner, lived in a house overlooking Falmouth Harbour, and he and Mrs. Dowman determined to buy the *Cutty* and preserve her as an example of superb ship-building. She was thoroughly overhauled and found to be as sound as when she was built in 1869, and then she was re-rigged as shown in the small drawing in Fig. 182. This, by the way, gives very little idea of the ship's beauty.

Perhaps the best thing to do would be to read Mr. Lubbock's book, " The Log of the *Cutty Sark*," to get an idea of what she did, and imagine her with all her sails set racing home under Captain Woodget's command from Sydney in sixty-seven days.

However, the *Cutty Sark* has made one more voyage— her last—to start a fresh and very individual career of usefulness, and rest for good at the mouth of the Thames, her home river in the days of her great voyages. She has now been appointed a successor to the famous old H.M.S. *Worcester*, which for many years trained young officers for the merchant navy, off Greenhithe, and lately sank at her moorings. Freshly painted and fitted, and manned by *Worcester* cadets, she was towed round from Falmouth under the command of Commander Steele, V.C., R.N., the Captain-Superintendent of the *Worcester*, and very fittingly Captain Dowman's son was on board. Is it not a fitting fate for this lovely creation of man's hands and skill, and will not those who read these lines go down to admire her as she lies at her anchored rest, with the ships of all nations passing up and down ?

We include three coloured plates of sailing ships; one is of vessels in the Canton River, China, with the East India-man *Waterloo* (Fig. 181) with her elaborate stern. She was of earlier type like the vessels of Nelson's day, and had a short life—let us hope it was a merry one! The *Joseph Cunard* (Fig. 184) was a barque, that is, she had no square sails or yards on the mizzen-mast. She was only half the size of the *Waterloo* or two-thirds of *Cutty*, but crossed the Atlantic to New Orleans and later sailed to India.

The third plate (Fig. 187) we are glad to include, as it shows from a water-colour a fully-rigged tea clipper under full sail. The *Spindrift* was built on the Clyde in 1867 and wrecked two years after, in the year the *Cutty Sark* came into being. We have been able to ascertain her tonnage, which is given as 899.

It is one of the most remarkable things in the history of navigation, this rise of the clipper ships both sides of the Atlantic; at its last hour the sailing vessel attained its perfection of design, and made its fastest passages forty years after steamers started regular ocean runs.

To mention just a few other famous clippers: there were the *Ariel*, *Taeping* and *Serica*, which had a famous race from China in 1866, and made the passage in ninety-nine days. Then there was the *Thermopylæ*, and *Sir Lancelot*, of 886 tons, with a crew of thirty and a canvas spread of

FIG. 185.—The U.S. Mail Steamship *Humboldt*, built at New York, 1850.

From Bowen's " The Sea : Its History & Romance " (Hatton & Co.)

By Lemercier.

over an acre. One of these ships sailed 1000 miles in three
days, and the *Taeping* and her fellows averaged thirteen
knots over long periods.

It was a magnificent swan-song, but it could not last.
The Suez Canal was opened in the *Cutty's* birth year, and
as steamers increased in size, with more reliable and
speedier engines of triple expansion type, the economic
scales were too heavily weighted against the windjammer,
and the future of carrying traffic, cargo and passenger,
passed for good to the engineer.

EMIGRATION.—There were great developments in transport during the nineteenth century because of emigration.
We have seen (p. 122) how Cobbett remarked, the "sensible fellows," with a little money, who packed up their
traps and went Westward Ho—400 from Norfolk in 1830,
and this was going on all over the northern part of Europe.

Wherever the steam engine and industrialism went
it meant a great dislocation of existing conditions and a
break in the traditions of life, and the land was full of
enmities and strife. Let us try and imagine the frame of
mind of one of the " sensible fellows " of 1830 in Norfolk ;
perhaps he was a hand-loom weaver from Norwich who
found his occupation gone, or a ploughwright who could no
longer make ploughs like Fig. 85, or one of those men who
had lost their holdings through the enclosures. Then
letters began to find their way back from America, and
tales were told in the inn of this great New World where
land could be had for the asking, and men were free and
the pursuit of happiness possible.

To help us into the frame of mind of the nineteenth-
century emigrants let us take an atlas to give us an idea
of the size of America, which it is so easy to forget. Take
a pair of compasses and place one leg round about Boston,
and stretch the other across the continent to Vancouver
Island ; now take the compasses and place one leg on
Brest, in the west of Brittany, and you will find the other
spans to the east of the Caspian Sea. In this vast area

were all the animal, vegetable and mineral riches which man desires, and they were to be had for the asking.

The growth of the United States can be seen by looking up the dates of the constitution of the various States. Here is a list. The government of the original thirteen on the Eastern Seaboard was ratified round about 1787-88 and 1789. Then followed Kentucky (1792), Tennessee (1796), Ohio (1803), Louisiana (1812), Indianapolis (1816), Mississippi (1817), Illinois (1818), Alabama (1819), Missouri (1821). Then Arkansas became a State in 1836, Michigan 1837, Florida and Texas 1845, Iowa 1846, Wisconsin 1848, and California 1850. That is to say that by the time of our Great Exhibition in 1851 roughly only one-half of the country was settled in States, and in the remainder the hardy pioneer and frontiersman were pushing out into the wilderness.

This peaceful penetration of a great continent is one of the miracles of history. Coming back from America on a great liner a few years ago we passed a schooner going to the fishing on the Newfoundland Banks—the merest cockle-shell of a boat—and the men waved to us, and we waved back, and thought at the time of the hardihood of the small crew, and then of all the other crews that have sailed across in every variety of ship, with all their possessions and full of hope—sensible if you like, and very courageous.

Which brings us to our next point—the influence all this movement was to have on the Old World, because it stands to reason that you cannot found a new world and expect the old one to remain the same. It is a sound mechanical law that if you exert a force in one direction, a reaction is set up in another.

Let us now follow our " sensible fellows " to America in 1830—the carpenters, wheelwrights, millwrights, smiths and bricklayers. When they arrived people were beginning to be interested in the Pacific coast as a place for settlement, and the Oregon Trail, a great unmade road 2000 miles long, from Independence to Oregon City, was being worn

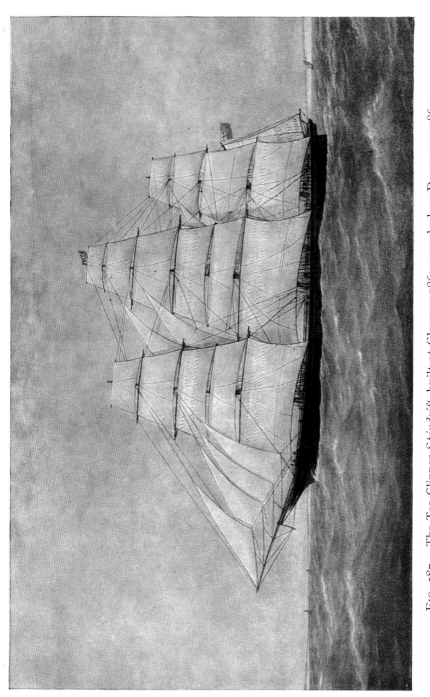

FIG. 187.—The Tea Clipper *Spindrift*, built at Glasgow 1867, wrecked on Dungeness 1869.

smooth by the waggon-wheels of the immigrants, and our
sensible fellows, if they went this way, would have been
pioneers, because thousands followed them. Nothing like
it has ever been seen before—nothing like it can ever
happen again. Where our friends went we cannot say,
but wherever it was—the Pacific Coast or one of the
frontier States—they would have found that they were
in a land without any traditions. At home, before the
coming of Industrialism, there had been no reason to do
a thing very quickly; if you built a waggon you did it
as well as you could and made it to last 100 years. Mass
production would have been ridiculous in a village or
country town. But when he got to the States man was
pigmy when compared with the countryside. It was not
a question of 100 men doing the work of 100 men, but 100
men confronted with the possibilities of employment for
thousands. It was a virgin country; all you had to do
was to walk in and help yourself with two hands and wish
you had twenty. So all the old traditions were cast on
one side and every possibility was explored for saving
labour. A perfectly proper thing to do.

Then there were the women to be considered, and
though we hear much of the Pilgrim Fathers, not so much
is said of the Pilgrim Mothers, yet they exercised an
enormous influence. No race of women ever played a
greater part in history than the wives and mothers who
followed the trail in the covered waggon, and bred a new
race and did all the chores at the same time. Had they
stayed at home and lived in such a house as we have
described in Chapter II they would have found their joy
in running their houses as we have described; but in a
new world this was not possible, and so the ingenuity of
their menfolk went to providing them with every labour-
saving appliance that would ease their unremitting toil.
Labour-saving was necessary in the New World, where the
frontier was always ahead, but it was a fatal doctrine for the
over-populated Old World, and it may even be that, now

the frontier of the New World has been reached, they too may have to consider whether Quantity is better than Quality.

ELECTRICITY.—The last name that we shall mention in this book is that of Michael Faraday (1791–1867), who in 1831, by his discovery of electro-magnetic induction, brought electricity into use. Faraday was a blacksmith's son, who left school at thirteen and began work by selling newspapers. His opportunity came when, after attending lectures by Sir Humphrey Davy, he called on the lecturer with his notes, and as a result was appointed a laboratory assistant at the Royal Institution at 25s. a week.

There is hardly a modern development in electrical engineering which cannot be traced back to Faraday. Many men followed in his footsteps ; Joseph Henry, an American, nearly anticipated Faraday's discovery. Lord Kelvin was the pioneer of submarine telegraphy ; James Clerk Maxwell put the discoveries into mathematical form ; Charles Wheatstone's experiments led to the electric telegraph ; David Edward Hughes invented the microphone ; Joseph Wilson Swan the incandescent filament lamp ; and Thomas Alva Edison is another name in the brilliant band—and the end is not yet. The latest development of Faraday's discovery is the distribution of electric power by means of the Grid in England, and it may be the most important.

Through the kindness of Mr. J. H. R. Body and the Newcomen Society we give some particulars of early electro-magnetic engines, from an interesting paper read by him recently before the Society. William Sturgeon evolved the electro-magnet in 1825 and seven years later he designed a machine in which a central shaft carrying two horizontal permanent bar magnets was made to revolve between four vertical electro-magnets energised with current from a battery. A reproduction of this machine is in the Science Museum. Soon after Davenport, in America, made a rudimentary electric locomotive which is really more like an electric merry-go-round. A little

THE " WAYSIDE INN "

later Robert Davidson, of Aberdeen, made an electric locomotive which actually ran at four miles per hour on a stretch of the Edinburgh and Glasgow railway (Fig. 173), electro-magnetic engines were also designed in America by Cotton in 1846 and Farmer in 1847 (Figs. 174, 175). All these ingenious machines failed in competition with steam from the weight and cost of the batteries which supplied their power ; electric traction did not really become practicable until the invention and application of the dynamo, but these early experiments are of intense interest as precursors of the enormous present day developments in electric traction on rail and road.

Watt's steam engine gathered men together because they had to go where the power was, and so the industrial towns came into being; electric energy, cheaply distributed, may take men back to the village and the countryside.

This brings us to our CONCLUSION. What hope is there for boys and girls of fourteen to eighteen who may read this book and wish to find interesting and useful work?

Whether we like it or not, the world to-day is still accepting the American tradition of mass-production and labour-saving which came about owing to the conditions we described on p. 216. Some while ago we were talking to a Japanese and asked him why in his country they were abandoning their own charming ways of making things and following Western fashions. " Oh," he said, " we must have lifts and things ; we must all be like America."

This is a question of primary importance. We had an extraordinarily interesting trip to America some years ago to inspect factories. We got as far west as Detroit, the home of mass production. Everybody was prosperous—dollar bills were as evident as leaves in the autumn—yet it all seemed unreal to us, this monstrous factory development, and we were happier motoring through New England and dining at the "Wayside Inn."

If mass production is to continue there are fearful dangers ahead. Carried to its logical conclusion, it means

219

entirely automatic plants and very little work for anybody, and a dull grey world, with the " dole " for consolation.

Again, there is the argument that all these things must be accepted because of our export trade; but nowadays all the nations are sellers, not buyers. That wise old man Johnson, when he was travelling in Scotland with Boswell, told him, in 1773 : " Depend upon it, this rage of trade will destroy itself. You and I shall not see it ; but the time will come when there will be an end of it. Trade is like gaming. If a whole company are gamesters, play must cease ; for there is nothing to be won. When all nations are traders, there is nothing to be gained by trade, and it will stop first where it is brought to the greatest perfection. Then the proprietors of land will be the great men." This prophecy has not been fulfilled ; we realise that export trade is essential for our existence, and it is now being encouraged and stimulated in every way.

It may be thought by our readers that we detest machinery. This is not the case at all ; we are very interested in it. It is the products of machinery which are so generally detestable. We speak with some experience, because one of the authors, when young, spent a year in a carpenter's shop where all the work was done by hand. Anybody who has spent a long summer's day rip-sawing 2-inch deals or jack-planing English oak is in the mood to accept the assistance of the machine—but it is a dangerous master. In its place the machine is a useful servant, and if work can be so organized with its aid that men can find an interest in their work, well and good. Given cheap electric power, the small tradesman of the village might come to life again and restore the balance of life there. How is this to be done ?

The remedy is in the hands of our readers, who in a few years will be men and women, running the world themselves. Trade and industry cannot be changed by Acts of Parliament, but they can be stimulated and altered by Demand.

SAVING

Take the case of women, who really run the world. They are the great spenders, not spendthrifts. The married woman decides what food the family shall eat, guided somewhat by her husband's grumbles; she has a distinct say in house-building, as any architect with an experience of clients' wives knows, and the woman decides what clothes she and her children will wear, and drives her husband to his tailor when he becomes too tramp-like.

Now, after the end of a second world war, the housewives are suffering from the shortage of almost all those things which used to be on sale so plentifully in the shops. These shortages are caused by the lack of the goods which we might have been making during the war, and by the loss of our overseas investments, which used to enable us to buy freely from abroad, and they can only be made good by increased production at home and by the greatest possible trade between the nations.

Still, the time will come, perhaps not till the readers of this book have grown up, when the shops are once again full of things to buy, and woman, the great spender, will be able to choose once more between goods which are shoddy and ugly (although cheap) and goods which are well-made and well-designed (although perhaps a little dearer). What an important choice that will be. On it will depend not only whether each home is individual, with furnishings of every kind which are good to look at and good in use, but also, what is even more important, it will decide the kind of work which we do to earn our living. If the choice goes in favour of goods which are sound and attractive we shall be able to do work in the making of them which will be a source of satisfaction and pride, as we all know that work may be, and not a mere day to day drudgery. In the meantime we must hope that the day will not be long delayed before such a choice again becomes possible.

N.B.—We have continued the tale in Vol. IV of this series which deals with Everyday Things from 1851 to 1914.

INDEX

The numerals indicated in black type refer to the illustrations, which are referred to under their **figure-numbers.**

INDEX

INDEX

INDEX

225

INDEX

Squire and parson, 38
Stage-coaches, **32, 32**B
Staircases, **35, 37,** 43, 46
Steamboats, 123, **185, 186,** 209
Steam coaches, **163, 164,** 202, 205
Steam engine, 82
Steam omnibus, **163, 167**
Steam power, 80
Stephenson, George, 207
Stoves, 31
Strand, the, 7
Straw plaiting, 120
Strawberry Hill, **37,** 48
Street, A. G., 147
Stuart, " Athenian," 59
Suburbs, **22**
Surgeons, 84
Sweeps, 34

Table, **126**
Table-ware, 29
Tailings, 131
Tailor, **151**
Taxes, 85, 114
Tea, 29
Telford, 198
Textiles, pre-factory, 8
Threshing, 27, **89, 90,** 120, 129
Tijou, Jean, 40
Tillage, 11
Timber carriage, **98,** 146
Timber truck, **99,** 146
Tips, 28, 30
Tithes, 27
" Tom Brown's Schooldays," 201
Town-planning, 82, 164
Towns, 3, **101, 102,** 164, 183
Townshend, 21
Traffic, **105**
Trains, **165, 166, 180**
Trams, 205
Transport, 77, 134, 198
Traps, drain, 97
Travelling, 7, 78, 198
Trenchers, **19,** 29
Trevithick, 204
Trevithick's model, **172**
Trough, **6**
Trousers, 196
Truck System, 123
Tull, Jethro, 3, 10, 20, 116
Tumbrils, **92, 93**
Turnips, 20, 26
Turnpikes, 122, 198
Turnspit, **20, 23**

Typhoid, 101
Typhus, 85

Vaccination, 83
Vails, 28, 30
Valve closets, **77,** 96
Valves, ball, 93
Vehicles (*v.* coaches, omnibus, steam, etc.), 78, 198
Viaduct, **74**
Victoria Embankment, 106
Viking ship, 135
Village amusements, **159, 160**
Villas, **112**

Wages, 25, 30, 109, 120, 123
Waggons, **31, 92, 94, 95, 96,** 135, **163**
Waistline, 193
Wallpapers, 50
Walpole, Horace, 148
Warp, 66
Washing, 33
Washington, George, 23
Waste or Common, 4
Water frames, 70
Water mills, 120
Water pipes, 93
Water supply, 90, 92, 166
" Waterloo," East Indiaman, **181**
Watt, James, 10, 80, 203
Weaving, **47, 49,** 63, 66, **149,** 184
Wedgwood, 51
Well winch, **75**
Wells, 92
Westminster, 104
Wheat, 27, 109, 119
Wheels, 136
Wheelwright, **97,** 136
Whiskers, 196
" William Fawcett," the, **183**
Windmills, 132
Window tax, 85
Winnowing, **91,** 130
Witney, 121
Woodforde Diary, 9, 24, 73, 83, 109
Woodforde, James, 24, 27, 78, 109
Woodforde, Nancy, 29, 33
Woodget, Capt., 212
Woodlands, 116
Woodwork, 43
Wren, 40
Wyatt, James, 149

Young, Arthur, 23, 25, 120

226